did not forbid. That is for another day, perhaps, in another, more expanded text.

I'm indebted to the following for inspiration, conversation, interviews and email exchange: David Toop, Dan Fox, Clive Bell, Rob Young, Anne Hilde Neset, Tony Herrington, Chris Bohn, Mark Fisher, Derek Walmsley and all the good people at *The Wire* magazine, Peter Rehberg, Christoph Cox, Simon Reynolds, Brian Duffy, Gurbir Thethy, Richard Beaudoin, Alex Ross, The Juneau Project, Throbbing Gristle.

FEAR OF MUSIC

WHY PEOPLE GET ROTHKO BUT DON'T GET STOCKHAUSEN

David Stubbs

zer0 books

London, UK
Washington, DC, USA

CollectiveInk

First published by Zero Books, 2009
Second edition published by Zero Books, 2024
Zer0 Books is an imprint of Collective Ink Ltd.,
Unit 11, Shepperton House, 89 Shepperton Road, London, N1 3DF
office@collectiveinkbooks.com
www.collectiveinkbooks.com
www.zero-books.net

For distributor details and how to order please visit the 'Ordering' section on our website.

Paperback ISBN: 978 1 80341 760 8
eBook ISBN: 978 1 80341 761 5
PCN: 2024930233

A CIP catalogue record for this book is available from the British Library.

Design credit(s): Lapiz Digital Services

UK: Printed and bound by CPI Group (UK) Ltd, Croydon, CR0 4YY
Printed in North America by CPI GPS partners

CONTENTS

INTRODUCTION

The idea which, in turn, formed the basis for this book came to me while I was watching, for perhaps the dozenth time, the Tony Hancock film *The Rebel*. He's being escorted around the palatial mansion of a wealthy French artist when he glances up at a piece of abstract expressionist art and exclaims, "Who's gone raving mad here, then?"

There are chortles all around, for although this film was released in 1961, it was understood even then that people of taste did not make such silly, Philistine remarks. It was understood that this piece of art was the product of rational meditation on the part of the artist, then duly submitted to an apparatus of critical approval, physical and cultural framing, exhibition and dealership, before being laid to rest, hung high on a wall, an elevated watermark of progressive, civilised thinking. "Raving mad"? Don't be a fool.

It then occurred to me how often the word "madness" is lazily invoked when those fully aware of the Pollocks and Rothkos of this world encounter, by chance, the works of experimental and avant-garde musicians, of whose activities they are only dimly aware. This happens to me all the time, among good and educated friends and acquaintances of mine — it's perfectly socially acceptable behaviour.

Why has avant-garde music failed to attain the audience, the cachet, the legitimacy of its visual equivalent?

There are a number of reasons for this which I shall go on to explore, but it's the "madness" thing that sticks in my own craw. Although some experimental music involves dalliances with irrationalism and the occult, I would prefer to highlight the overwhelmingly rational and coherent reasons why a number of people have chosen to make, and to listen to, music which to uninitiated ears sounds cacophonous, atonal — "just noise". Some of this music has been accepted as legitimate; some of it remains beyond the pale. The people who make it, however, are in general perfectly willing and able to articulate just what it is they are trying to do and why they are doing it, rarely shuffling off and taking refuge in the sort of mumbled excuses about the "music speaking for itself", to which their pop contemporaries are more wont. Part of this book, therefore, is a history, albeit a potted and highly subjective one, of twentieth-century music set in its social and aesthetic contexts and in parallel with developments in the arts. This music happened for reasons.

I've also resented the somewhat feebly lobbed brickbats of derision which avant-garde music and its followers have perennially to endure. As a sometime comedy writer, the simplistic and persistent equation between a love of Stockhausen and chronic humourlessness is wearily offensive. So, every now and again, here and there, I've tried turning the gun carriage around on the mockers. The ones who, like Anthony Aloysius Hancock, still don't get it, even this late on, and whose own ideas of "art appreciation" are often based on discredited foundations.

This text isn't intended as a sealed and finished piece of academic work — it's as much a matter of questions, suspicions and impressions as answers, historical facts and conclusions. It's intended to tease and provoke further reflection, debate and disagreement rather than to settle any matter. It cannot do justice to the massive amount of twenty-first-century activity, in both art and music, which would merit inclusion in this volume if space

CHAPTER 1

SCHISM

October, 2007. The Tate Modern, London. Doris Salcedo's *Shibboleth* is on exhibition in the sloping, forbiddingly cavernous Turbine Hall. The *Shibboleth* consists of what appears to be a long, zig-zagging crack running through the floor of the hall, which grows from barely more than a scratch in the tiling at the hall's entrance to a much larger fissure, like a miniature canyon, some 30 or 40 metres wide at the point where most visitors congregate. As you enter the hall, attendants press leaflets into your hand, reading: "Warning: Please watch your step in the Turbine Hall. Please keep your children under supervision." Come the end of the year, and 19 lawsuits have been brought against the Tate Modern by visitors claiming to have been injured by this exhibit.

Today, however, nobody looks at all put out by the schism in the floor. The Tate Modern, very probably the UK's leading tourist destination, is packed, with practically every demographic, every continent, represented. Do a 360° swivel and they are all there. In the café seats overlooking the Turbine Hall, a pensioner munches diffidently on a damp sandwich. Slumped against the far wall are a couple of down-and-outs clutching warm tins of lager, taking in the human traffic. To and fro pass old Americans, young Europeans, huddles of women, single men, families with infants in buggies, retired couples, foreign students and excited school kids. One tourist and his wife dutifully read aloud in monotone the notes to *Shibboleth* in the leaflet forced on them, as if reading an instruction manual. "Walking down Salcedo's incised line … particularly if you know about her previous work, might well prompt a broader consideration of power's divisive operations as encoded in the brutal narratives of colonialism, their unhappy aftermaths in post-colonial nations, and in the stand-off between rich and poor, northern and southern hemispheres."

Now, here I observe an altogether different schism — between the notes and the reality out on the floor. People are enjoying Salcedo's exhibit, enjoying it thoroughly. They marvel aloud at the technical aspects, revere the leap of "creative imagination" it took to conceive of such a thing, such a breach beneath their very feet. They stand astride the schism and snap each other on their mobile phones and digital cameras. They stick their hands down the schism. Since the work of art in this particular case isn't a solid object but an absence of solid object, is that schism, that bit of fresh air they've just stuck their hands in, the work of art? Are they, therefore, in technical, naughty breach of the "Do Not Touch" rule, that invisible force field which still surrounds gallery art?

One young lad snatches his hand in and out, as if afraid that the curators have set up some sort of electric shock device for transgressors. What no one is doing, if their cheerful demeanour is anything to go by, is contemplating the brutal narratives of colonialism or their unhappy aftermaths in post-colonial nations. This is not because these good people are indifferent to colonialist brutality or its after-effects, or too stupid to make the connection. It is simply, one suspects, that the connection has been hitched on, as an act of piety, to validate and lend a proper conceptual gravitas to this particular artistic act, to satisfy the needs, spoken or otherwise, of everybody involved — the artist, the curator, the sponsors Unilever, the director of the Tate Modern, Sir Nicholas

Serota, even the visitors who are comforted to know that there is some latent, morally nutritious purpose to their joyride down this fissure, freeing them up to enjoy it — as spectacle, subversion, fun. And why not? There is, after all, insufficient data inscribed in the *Shibboleth* itself to make its ostensibly didactic purpose an effective one.

I amble around the rest of the gallery. I should say, I'm no man apart from the common herd, disdaining the unwashed populace gawping at these priceless works of which they have no comprehension. In the expressions of my fellow visitors, I detect the same mixture in them that's buoying me up and weighing me down — the barely stifled urge to yawn deeply, coupled with a sense of serenity and curiosity, a sense of mental cloudiness that no amount of forced concentration will dispel, coupled with the occasional, piercing shaft of epiphany and joy in the face of, say, a Chirico, the sense of having somehow been fed and watered at a deeper level, coupled with a craving for a cup of tea and a blueberry muffin. I tag onto a group being led around by a kindly in-house guide who explains in plain but not inaccurate terms the significance of the replica of Marcel Duchamp's urinal, signed "R. Mutt". Was the urinal violating the cordoned off, sacred space of the art gallery, or, more likely, freeing up ideas of what sort of thing was admissible in the gallery, and by whom? Another work, by recently deceased American minimalist artist Sol LeWitt, presents a new and special set of problems. The work consists of a matrix of white lines chalked in geometric and criss-cross fashion across a number of blackboards. What's most noteworthy is how this piece must be transported should another gallery, say, in Paris, wish to exhibit it. What would then happen is that workers at the Tate Modern would scrub out the lines on the boards they had erected, thereby erasing the work. It would then rematerialise in Paris, redrawn by their gallery's people, following strict instructions from the artist. The "work" here is not the physical thing but the "immaterial" concept, with great lengths travelled in order to preserve its sacrosanctness.

I stroll around the rest of the galleries, milling curiously, appreciatively, dutifully, rapt with boredom, fascinated and fatigued, just like everybody else — works by Luc Tuymans, Marlene Dumas, Fiona Rae. Some of the more abstract works, only decades old, seem dead and encrusted in their frames, like flattened-out fossils, products of a vanished, utopian era. I look at Max Ernsts's *Celebes*, with its docile, elephantine, machine-type figure beckoned away by a headless mannequin. In a moment of fleeting smugness, I recall looking at this same picture at the old Tate Gallery on Millbank, back in the mid-'80s, in relatively sparse company. But were those really better times?

The corridors of the Tate Modern are rife with marketing stratagems and messages designed to catch the corner of the eye. Apparently, "The Tate sends 250,000 email bulletins each month."

That's good, you suppose. And then there is a timeline, set out in the same perkily handwritten font as you see displayed outside the more whimsically minded coffee outlets at city railway stations. It's a timeline of modern art throughout the twentieth century and beyond, an inky shoal of the great and good swimming through the twentieth century and into the twenty-first — from Picasso to Rae, Chapman, Emin and even Christian Marclay and Mike Kelley, who cross over between the visual and sound arts. The time line is interspersed with reminders of what else was happening in the twentieth century at any given point, be it Josephine Baker, World War II, or The Beatles.

For many, the holy of holies of the Tate Modern is the Rothko Room, featuring the *Seagram Murals*. Assisted, unfairly perhaps, by being bathed in a half-light, Rothko's murals go some way to transcending the limits of the canvas, simulating the all-enveloping, dark ambient, abstract effects of a certain kind of music. Rothko speaks gloomily of emulating Michelangelo's Laurentian Library in Florence, constructed in the sixteenth century, and there's the same sense of being "trapped" in a chamber, in which total absorption is compulsory but the experience is deeply compelling. It's more than a hush that descends upon the random collection of strangers assembled briefly together in the presence of *Red on Maroon*. It's as if the painting is surpassing itself, emitting inaudible, cryptic but urgent drones. Brian Duffy, the sound artist and creator of "circuit-bending" avant-pop group The Modified Toy Orchestra, believes that the secret of Rothko is his supreme acumen in the abstract domain. "The first time I walked into the Rothko Room I felt depressed; but in fact, to be so in control of your medium as to get exactly the right frequency of light to make me feel depressed is a masterstroke, showing complete control of his medium. He's a craftsman of frequency. He's saying something that couldn't be said any other way."

Mark Rothko, like many artists, had a strong association with contemporary and comparative musicians of his day. John Cage had his Robert Rauschenberg; Rothko had his Morton Feldman, who wrote a beautiful commemorative piece on the opening of the Rothko Chapel in 1971 in Houston, Texas. What, then, of the Tate Modern's musical dimension? In the main shop, art, photography, cinema, sculpture, design, architecture, are all well represented in the books section, sternly overlooking the sillier plethora of souvenir scarves, mugs, etc. But music? Well, there's a solitary CD by Robin Rimbaud, aka Scanner, and a small selection of CDs on the LTM label, collating scratchy recordings of the futurists, interviews with surrealists and the like. And that is your lot.

The success of the Tate Modern, since its opening in 2000 on Bankside, is indisputable. Transformed from what was a miserably blackened, imposing but ignored husk of a former power station, it's now one of the vital engines in Thameside London's regeneration as one of Europe's main tourist attractions, linked by a new pedestrian bridge and nestled amid a flotilla of new restaurants. Much of its success is down to the dark, contemporary arts of marketing and (re)branding and to the enterprise and zeal of Nicholas Serota. It has a nice selection of drinking and dining options and commanding views. However, the Tate would not, could not, be the phenomenon it is today had there not been an acceptance by the general public of contemporary art in all its forms — abstract, conceptual, non-figurative, collage. You could send out all the emails you like, flag up the featured artists in as whimsical a font as you please, the Thames could be twinkling turquoise beneath you, but the precondition for getting people through those doors has to be a genuine desire on the part of a great many of them to come and see some avant-garde visual art. Their reasons for wanting to do so may be open to doubt and debate, the levels of their comprehension and appreciation varying, but what is beyond dispute is that the Tate is regularly crammed to the rafters because people haven't just learned to tolerate the likes of Pollock, Rothko and De Kooning — they're willing to give up their precious afternoons to come and behold their works. Sure, you will still find the odd, disgruntled voice of dissent in the letters pages of the *Telegraph*, the grandparent whose views on modern art are informed by 1970s *Daily Mail* articles fulminating against piles of bricks in galleries subsidised by the Arts Council, as well as the annual parade of huffing and snorting against some chap dressed as a bloody bear winning the Turner Prize. There are even the Stuckists who, with an eloquence and purpose not to be sniffed at, have set up their own rearguard action against the non-figurative tendencies of modern art. However, the fact is that it's commonly understood that it is simply not done; when confronted with a piece of abstract expressionist art, one might yelp, as did Tony Hancock in *The Rebel*, "Who's gone raving mad here, then?"

Contemporary art is headline news. When Hugh Grant sold his Andy Warhol portrait of Elizabeth Taylor in 1963 at a huge profit in 2007, it was all over the papers and TV for days. Granted, this was in part because of the triple whammy of celebrities involved — Hugh, Andy, Liz. However, in May of 2007, there was a series of record-breaking purchases of post-war art. Francis Bacon's portrait *Study from Innocent X* fetched $52.6m (£26.5m) at Sotheby's in New York — almost double the previous record for a Bacon work. There followed a price of $72.8m (£36.7m) for Mark Rothko's 1950 work *White Center (Yellow, Pink and Lavender on Rose)*. Fifteen artists saw new auction records set for their work, including Jean-Michel Basquiat, whose untitled work from 1981 fetched $14.6m (£7.4m), almost three times his previous best. This showed that, for whatever reasons, recognition of the value of contemporary art has come a long way since 1916, when Hans Arp, one of the first abstract artists, was commissioned to paint the entrance to a girls' school in Zurich. The principal was so appalled by the non-representative blobs of colour they offered that he at once ordered for the offending frescoes to be painted over with a mercifully figurative work entitled *Mothers, Leading Children by the Hand.*

Today, modern art is accepted at all levels, from pavement to penthouse corporate. But what has become of its musical equivalent? Both music and the visual arts entered modernity in the first decade of the twentieth century — modern art with Picasso's *Les Demoiselles D'Avignon*, in which one of the female sitters' faces looks to have been violently supplanted by some sort of African mask. Around the same time, Arnold Schoenberg is composing the very first of his "atonal" works, thereby bringing the whole harmonically developed structure of classical music crashing down. A few years later, Luigi Russolo writes his *Art of Noises* futurist manifesto; jazz's birth pangs and development, en route to its own "dissonance", become increasingly audible; via correspondence, Kandinsky and Schoenberg try to establish some sort of art-musical synaesthetic Gesamtkunstwerk.

And yet, today, their fates are very different. In his formidable survey of twentieth-century music *The Rest Is Noise*, *New Yorker* critic Alex Ross touches on this: "While the splattered abstractions of Jackson Pollock sell on the art market for a hundred million dollars or more [...] the equivalent in music still sends ripples of unease through concert audiences and makes little discernible impact on the outside world." The same people who flock from miles around to mill in the presence of abstract art run screaming, hands clasped to their ears like Munch females, from "abstract music". Well, perhaps that over-dramatises their response. More likely, on the rare and fleeting occasions on which they bump into such music, perhaps by accident on Resonance FM, they'll dismiss it with a "What's this racket? Turn it off!" or calmly operate the switch themselves, turning towards a more temperate destination on the dial.

A measure of contrasting contemporary attitudes towards the twin avant-gardes can be found in responses to the death of Karlheinz Stockhausen. The obituary writers gave him a respectable send-off, but Private Eye's EJ Thribb offered the following in memoriam:

So. Farewell
Then Karlheinz
Stockhausen.

Famous modern
Composer.

All together
Now —

Bing. Bang!
Three-minute silence
Knock. Knock.
Beep.
Plonk.
Bang!
Whirrr…

I hope I
Have got
This right.

Meanwhile, the *Guardian* obituary was followed up by a one-line letter from one of its correspondents suggesting that a fitting tribute to the late composer would be to stage one minute's cacophony.

All this could be added to a pile of similarly wheezily labouring mirth, much of which is collected, in cartoon form, on Stockhausen's own website. A 2004 cartoon in the *Guardian* shows a surgeon explaining to his patient on the operating table, "No, it's not Stockhausen — we've just dropped a tray of surgical instruments." One can only hope in all charity that there was some additional bit of context that might have made this even half funny at the time. Another shows a piano tuner asking the owner of the Steinway, "When did you first notice that your Mozart sounded like Stockhausen?" The late *Punch* magazine added a couple of their own. A jogger's curiously squiggly progress is explained by the fact that he is listening to Stockhausen on his Walkman. Another cartoon features upstairs neighbours pogoing about randomly and smashing a ping-pong ball hither and yon as their downstairs neighbours complain, "It sounds like those bloody idiots upstairs are playing their Stockhausen records again."

Now, there is nothing wrong, in principle, with anyone taking an irreverent dig at the High Arts. It does little to abate the smirkers, it must be said, when the press release on Stockhausen's demise contains the following sentiment, penned by one of his adorers: "On December 5th he ascended with JOY through HEAVEN'S DOOR, in order to continue to compose in PARADISE with COSMIC PULSES in eternal HARMONY, as he had always hoped to do." However, the jokes I cite above I found offensive, not as a lover of avant-garde music but as a lover of comedy. They are feeble — but it is such a cultural given, a default setting, that Stockhausen be automatically derided, that no one apparently feels the need to work very hard at the quality of jokes at his expense. Stockhausen, you see, is a joke — or so goes the (un)thinking.

Modern art has long since ceased to be the common butt of such jibes. Sure, there have been hoaxers and pranksters over the years, such as "Bruno Hat", the 1929 modern art creation of Evelyn Waugh and a handful of his cohorts, and in more recent times, the "neo neos", created by *Spy* magazine, who put on an exhibition of work akin to the "Infantile" school of art created by scriptwriters

Ray Galton and Alan Simpson for Tony Hancock's *The Rebel.* But when, in a 1980s episode of *Minder*, Arthur Daley converses with a crooked art dealer and espouses his own, unwittingly Stuckist theories of painting, "I like pigs, sheeps, goats — y'know, proper pictures," the joke is clearly on Daley, the Sarf London après-garde Philistine, not the art dealer.

Modern music feels decades away from such acceptance. Had Arthur Daley remarked that he liked "songs — you know, tunes, harmonies, that sort of thing — proper music," he would be roundly applauded as a voice of common sanity in some quarters by a world supposedly dominated by the agenda of Radio 3 elitist atonalists, zealots deaf not just to what constitutes good music but also to the wishes of ordinary people.

Stockhausen was, indeed, as EJ Thribb laconically observes, a "famous modern composer", and the fact that he was able to enjoy a prolonged career and pack concert halls indicates for some the triumph of contemporary music. Certainly, he owes his pre-eminence not just to a sense of the dramatic when it came to promoting his ideas but also to the innate sense of drama, the symphonic sweep which elevates his masterpieces above the vast majority of musique concrète.

However, for many, Stockhausen is "the only one", the sole household name or signifier of twentieth-century experimental music and therefore perceived as a lone eccentric, an aberrant, isolated figure orbiting Earth pointlessly like a rusty old Sputnik, a relic of futurisms past. That he is merely one prominent and lofty figure in a largely undersea mountainscape is hardly ever recognised. What of Pierre Schaeffer, Iannis Xenakis, Gyorgy Ligeti, Luc Ferrari, Herbert Eimert, Pierre Henry, Nicolas Schöffer, Henri Pousseur, Bruno Maderna, to name just a few in his own field? Broaden the focus to other genres and it would be easy to make of these pages a giant directory, or index of activity, from Salvatore Sciarrino to William Basinski, from Sun Ra to Merzbow, from Sightings to Albert Ayler, from Pere Ubu to Burial, from AMM to Faust. To anyone with a subscription to the magazine *The*

Wire, these are common enough names. However, to a disturbing number of people with culture and education bursting from their ears, they are utterly unknown. There are prominent figures in the world of contemporary art — it would be unfair to name names — who are known simply to have no idea what has been going on in contemporary music, in the realms beyond rock and roll, pop, and mainstream jazz and classical. Such ignorance is the equivalent of an experimental or avant-garde musician whose tastes in art ran to framed depictions of dogs playing billiards and poker.

Furthermore, there isn't much demonstration of will on the part of modern art's major urban cathedrals to stress the links between the contemporary art they frame and comparative developments in contemporary music. The Tate Modern's timeline makes no such allusions, feels no need to do so. Instead, modern art's trajectory is shown against a backdrop of pop-historical and sociological trends. Meanwhile, a CD on sale at New York's Guggenheim Museum entitled *Raising the Standards* offers a companion in sound to the museum's permanent collection of Kandinskys, Picassos, etc., consisting of smart jazz renditions from the late bebop era, with versions of standards such as *How High the Moon* played by the likes of André Previn, Kenny Burrell and Stan Getz. This feels more designed to evoke for consumers a halcyon era of '50s Manhattan midtown metropolitan smartness, when New York enjoyed its status as a new centre of the modern art world, than to map any parallel developments in contemporary experimental music. (An honourable exception to all this is the Centre Pompidou, whose 2004 exhibition *Sons et Lumières* showed the ways in which, in the early twentieth century in particular, modern art and modern music had cross-fertilised).

Of course, it is not the primary job of the visual art galleries to promote the cause of avant-garde music, though given recent, post-Fluxus developments in sound art, for instance, you might expect them to be less oblivious to its very existence. But let's have a look at another indicator — *The South Bank Show*, whose brief has always been to bring the arts to a more mainstream audience. Scrolling down a list of its weekly topics since its inception in 1978, let's see how twentieth-century experimental art and twentieth-century experimental music fare in a head-to-head.

Given the Melvyn Bragg treatment have been the surrealists, David Hockney (three times), Frank Auerbach, Graham Sutherland, Howard Hodgkin (twice), Soviet Art, Patrick Caulfield, Marc Chagall, Francis Bacon, Patrick Heron, Arthur Boyd, Jackson Pollock, Wendy Taylor, Nicola Hicks, Roy Lichtenstein, Paula Rego, Jeff Koons, The Guggenheim Museum, Christian Boltanski, Claes Oldenburg, Andy Warhol, Picasso, Gilbert And George, Yoko Ono, Chuck Close, Marlene Dumas, Marc Quinn, Tracey Emin, Rachel Whiteread, Sophie Calle, Peter Blake, Grayson Perry.

This list excludes the likes of Maggi Hambling and Andrew Wyeth, who are primarily figurative artists, a minority in twentieth- and twenty-first-century art. Maybe Hockney can be excluded on this basis too.

Now let's look at the roll call of twentieth-century experimental music covered by The South Bank Show over these last 30 years. Michael Tippett, Benjamin Britten, Alban Berg, Peter Maxwell Davies, Stravinsky, Miles Davis, Vaughan Williams, a one-hour feature on "Electronic music", Messaien's *Turangalîla-Symphonie*, Phillip Glass, Jimi Hendrix, Henze, Hindemith, John Adams, John Tavener, Steve Reich.

Not much of a haul. What's more, "experimental" is rather a stretch with some of these selections, which largely represent the British, the palatable, or the minimalist, holy or otherwise. Minimalism is among the most favoured and commercially successful form of modern music — when the new Eurostar station at St Pancras was unveiled in TV adverts, the soundtrack was, inevitably, a bowdlerised take on minimalism, a latticed, oscillating orchestral arrangement which bespoke both high class and easy access for the listener. Music as a whole has been well represented on The South Bank Show over the years, but far greater primacy is given to performers, particularly vocalists, whose repertoire is predominantly pre-twentieth-century rather than contemporary composers. They have the advantage of being alive, engaged in classical music but not inconveniently bound up solely with modernity. Pop and rock music are also well represented — Sting, Paul McCartney, Eric Clapton, Annie Lennox, George Michael, as well as the likes of Andrew Lloyd Webber. Load in those plus Bernie Taupin, Elton John's lyrical collaborator, and "modern music", in the sense of music made in modern times, feels pretty well catered for. However, the predominant, popular modes of modern music have confined themselves — for good, sound commercial reasons — to orthodox, strictly tonal contours. This is in contrast to the visual arts. The lonely, self-pitying figure of Jack Vettriano, he of the dancing butlers, can justly feel isolated in that he is one of the few prominent contemporary artistic figures to eschew avant-garde methods — and is derided for his obdurate, trite, anti-modernity.

Still, at least he is represented. Where, by contrast, is Derek Bailey, a towering figure in the history of British free-improvised music? One scrolls down the South Bank roll of honour in vain. David Bailey, yes, and Derek Walcott the following week in 1988, but no Derek Bailey. Bernie Taupin, yes, but Derek Bailey, no.

In fairness, such an oversight probably represents the commercial realities faced by the makers of the *SBS*. But the upshot is that despite their overall strong emphasis on music, especially on classical performers, modern experimental music has never gone beyond the thin end of the wedge. It is forced to flourish, like hyacinths, in the darkness, its practitioners, when fleetingly observed, imagined to be engaged in some sort of morbidly obscure madness. Writer and musician Clive Bell recalls a recent experience, watching David Toop's Laptop Orchestra, a workshop project organised with students of his, a group who improvise by using computer-processed sounds.

"They were invited to play to an audience of psychoanalysts, down in South London," recalls Bell. "They were from various disciplines — Jung, Lacan, Freud. I knew one of them, so

I went down too. The idea was that the Laptop Orchestra would play, then there would be some discussion, then they would play again, so that they could talk about the interaction between the group and see if there was anything interesting happening from a psychological point of view. I think the event perhaps wasn't very well set up because nobody explained at the beginning what the group did. And it soon became clear that this audience, this very nice, highly educated audience hadn't got the foggiest idea what was going on. It was a double whammy of ignorance. Not only were they completely unfamiliar with the idea of free improvisation, but they'd never seen anyone make music with a laptop. So they couldn't grasp what might be going on there — which I agree is weird, because you can't see what's physically going on. They couldn't get into it at all. And they started talking about it as if it was very freakish, very marginal behaviour they were witnessing. People were even talking in terms of insanity."

It's comical to think of these psychoanalysts fulminating uncomprehendingly, like latter-day versions of PG Wodehouse's Sir Roderick Glossop, the Harley Street "nerve specialist" who, when greeted with the alien high jinks of Bertie Wooster's lively circle of young things, ascribes their behaviour to mental disorder. But sad, also, because it signals the lack of recognition afforded to a vast, legitimate, logical, continuing, creative but attention-starved sphere of human activity. The most recent victim is the London Musician's Collective, who organise events and releases involving experimental musicians from all around the world. Despite the Arts Council having enjoyed a boost to its coffers, in 2007 they nonetheless announced a swingeing round of cuts. Among their victims was the LMC, but among the beneficiaries, by contrast, were the visual arts.

Although experimental art and experimental music do end up unwillingly "competing" for resources, they do not compete in any other sense. Any opposition implied in the title of this book is a false one — the two are not really at odds with each other.

There are numerous artists who work in both disciplines — there is common ground, common sympathy, there are common problems and common aesthetics. So why can the general public apparently not get enough of one avant-garde and yet barely be aware of the existence of the other? Why the schism?

CHAPTER 2

THE ART OF NOISE, THE NOISE OF ART

There may never again be a new century that dawns with such gathering turbulence, such an impending promise and threat, such a strong, electric inkling of collapse and rebirth in the offing, so palpable a sense that the doors of perception were hanging off their hinges, like there was at the beginning of the twentieth. The Millennium Bug was a pretty damp squib by comparison. At the end of the nineteenth century, Christianity, or at least the base assumptions about human behaviour and morality it represented, was rocking on its plinth, under assault from both Darwin and Nietzsche. Freud published *The Interpretation of Dreams* in 1900. One point upon which these intellectual giants converged was that God, and the brittle hierarchy and explanations he represented, was about to be supplanted from below by a new reckoning of long-latent human energies, the first scent of which was caught by the Romantics. Yet the Romantics would have been horrified at the denuding of the "natural" landscape, sucked dry by the Industrial Revolution, and the beginnings of the mechanised, economically expanding society that we continue, at least for the time being, to enjoy. The emergence of a new, teeming, lower middle class alarmed both the radical/literary and the arch conservative wings of the old elite. Meanwhile, the old European Empires were now locked together in a complex and precarious over-development of treaties, agreements and alliances which would result in the absurdity of one hot-headed young Serb who couldn't even get his street directions right, popping a gun and bringing Europe and the rest of the world crashing into cataclysm. Only the futurists unambiguously heralded the dynamic new century, its horrors as well as its exhilarations. "We will glorify war," wrote Marinetti, "The world's only hygiene." He got his wish, of course, as the ancients who directed the First World War blithely sent so many young men to their deaths, as if out of subconscious vindictiveness towards their impertinent juniors and the new world they potentially represented — the nineteenth century's last act of vengefulness against the twentieth, using the new century's own mechanical means.

Certainly, it was absolute disgust with the carnage of World War I which prompted the beginnings of the Dada movement in Zurich in 1916 and their desire to tear up the sacred tenets of a civilisation which had recoiled, as a result of its own overreaching logic, into barbarism. Here was an art movement, which, like futurism several years earlier, was born directly and explicitly out of a political context.

The departure from tonality in cubism and Schoenberg represents the birth of visual and musical modernity. It arose from their two chosen art forms breaking down, in some ominous parallel with civilisation as a whole, under the rules of their own continued "growth and development". Visual art was put under pressure to change in a way that music wasn't — by the rise of photography, which, to anyone who could read the writing on the wall, promised to render figurative representation in art largely obsolete. With the camera now taking up the role once played by the brush and canvas, it is perfectly understandable why Picasso should have taken up the initiative from first the impressionists, then Cezanne, making the logical leap into the realms of "non-representation", from the figurative into the abstract, from the objective to the subjective, the fundamental shift of modernity. It's not hard to see how and why this hop, step and jump took place.

Schoenberg's reaction against nineteenth-century music — which had culminated in the gargantuan, symphonic swansong of Wagner — is less easy to divine; indeed, 100 years on, he remains a symbol of musical opacity for many, derided as obsolete by some, unexplored by others, the Godfather of "difficulty" in modern music. Even today, some commentators vaguely ascribe his abandonment of tonality to some sort of wilful contrarianism, an arbitrary and perverse fit of liberal elitism of a piece with the impulse that prompted Eliot to write *The Waste Land*, a deliberate attempt to hoist art to some impossibly high sanctuary, away from the grubby grasp of the increasing hordes which would come to be known as the masses.

Although Schoenberg was turning inward, he was motivated by idealism, albeit one he chose to express exclusively in artistic means. He loved Mahler, his mentor, but saw that if classical music was to continue to evolve, he would have to write in a mode which the Mahlers of this world would find impossible to understand.

For some, Schoenberg is a repressive figure, the twelve tone system of music he first put forward in 1923 locking modern classical music into a sort of "compulsory democracy". They consider the system's precise intervals and mandatory use of all the twelve pitch class numbers in varying sequences to be a cerebral exercise in composition designed to achieve maximum dissonance and unlistenability. He wasn't throwing out the rulebook but introducing a stricter one. His systemic desire to avoid repetition at all costs — repetition represented regression — makes him sound alien to modern ears, steeped as they are in minimalism and repetition. But Schoenberg's desire was to liberate the hitherto repressed properties of musical sound. In his *Harmonielehre*, Schoenberg advanced further the ideas wishfully mooted by Alexander Scriabin in his works for "colour organ". He wrote that although pitch had previously been measured in music, colour and intensity had not. By laying a proper and systematic stress on those qualities, Schoenberg hoped, and indeed succeeded, to lay down the foundations for a music which would give full vent and expression to the dreams, inner impulses, visions and utopian ideals of the composer. Yes, it might seem strange and dissonant, but as he himself wrote, dissonances were merely "remoter consonances".

Meanwhile, in painting, the abstract expressionists were thinking along the same lines. "When the external supports threaten to collapse, then man's gaze turns away from the external towards himself," wrote Wassily Kandinsky. Just as he was a musician of some talent, a cellist and pianist, so Schoenberg exhibited his own canvases. In 1910, the year Schoenberg wrote *Harmonielehre*, Kandinsky wrote his own tract, *On the Spiritual in Art*. Kandinsky was producing the first abstract watercolours at the same time Schoenberg was doing away with tonality. Both men, it turned out, had dreams of a Gesamtkunstwerk, a theatrical piece perhaps, in which the spiritual qualities of the new music and painting of the twentieth century could come together in glorious synthesis, something of which Kandinsky had first had an inkling on being exposed to Wagner. After Kandinsky then witnessed a performance of Schoenberg's *Three Piano Pieces* in 1911, he and the composer struck up an excited correspondence in which each mirrored the ideas of the other. "This human tendency towards the fossilising of form is shocking, even tragic," wrote Kandinsky. Schoenberg, in turn, declared that "Every formal procedure which aspires to traditional effects is not completely free from conscious motivation. But art belongs to the unconscious! One must express oneself! Express oneself directly! Not one's taste, not one's upbringing, or one's intelligence, knowledge, or skill. Not all those acquired characteristics but that which is inborn, instinctive!" Here, he gets to the nub of what both men passionately sought — a mainline to the inner self, the fertile fields of the "unconscious" whose existence Freud had established, in which new worlds could be conceived of without hindrance from old forms and conventions which had come to exist merely for their own sake. Schoenberg thanked Kandinsky profusely for a selection of pictures he sent him. He drew particular succour from their colour, "not 'beautiful' colour but colour which is expressive in its relationships." Kandinsky, meanwhile, wrote to Schoenberg, "You have realised what I [...] have so greatly longed for in music. The independent progress through their own destinies, the independent life of the individual voices in your compositions is exactly what I am trying to find in my paintings." Kandinsky, envious of music's exemplary status as the only true "abstract" art, sought to find a way of assigning "sound values" to each colour in the spectrum (the trumpet for yellow, etc.) as a compositional aid on the canvas. The synaesthetic sparks that fly up as these two towering forefathers of modernity rub along so well together still fire up the spirits today. Put simply, Schoenberg was trying to make music that aspired to possess the qualities of painting; Kandinsky was painting pictures that truly followed Walter Pater's dictum in aspiring to the condition of music. To listen to Schoenberg would be to hear colour, to look at Kandinsky would be to see sound.

However, it never quite happened. The relationship faltered in the early 1920s when Schoenberg, of relatively lowly Viennese stock, accused the upper middle-class orthodox Russian, Kandinsky, of having expressed anti-Semitic sentiments when the artist alluded, albeit in inverted commas, to the supposed "Jewish problem". In his shocked defence, Kandinsky may inadvertently have made things a little worse for himself. He tried to hail Schoenberg, in a manner reminiscent of Nietzsche, as a kindred spirit in a higher stratosphere above and beyond mere petty ethnic differences. On 24 April 1923, he wrote to the composer, "It is no great fortune to be a Jew, Russian, German, European. Better to be a human being. But we should strive to be 'supermen'!" He also protested, "You have a frightful picture of the 'Kandinsky of today'. I reject you as a Jew but nevertheless I write you a good letter and assure you that I would be so glad to have you here in order to work together!" The line "I reject you as a Jew" was most probably meant as an ironic representation by Kandinsky of how Schoenberg felt slighted. That's the only way it makes sense in the context of the painter's clear desire to maintain a friendship with Schoenberg. However, the composer appeared to take the line literally in a lengthy response, the last correspondence between the two men for five years: "You join in that sort of thing and 'reject me as a Jew'. Did I ever offer myself to you?" However, the remainder of the letter stands as an indictment of a mounting anti-Semitism in Germany and Austria, which may have clouded Schoenberg's vision as regards Kandinsky's feelings towards him but stands as a clear-eyed vision of things as they were and things to come in his neck of Europe for the Jewish people — the more astonishing in its clarity, since Schoenberg was viewed as a dry and hermetic figure who took refuge in art's "inner world" from the realities of human existence. Alluding briefly to Hitler, ten full years before he became Chancellor, he senses the prospect of the prevailing mood of anti-Semitism leading to "acts of violence" and foresees the same "rivers of blood" that flowed under the birth pangs of communism, as well as anticipating Jews being deprived of their civil rights.

It's now believed that Alma Mahler-Werfel, daughter of Gustav Mahler and later wife of Walter Gropius, founder of the Bauhaus movement, had a malicious hand in stoking Schoenberg's grievance against Kandinsky. They did meet again and occasionally corresponded, but never with the same fervour. Whether they would have arrived at any great synthesis had it not been for the interruption of world affairs is debatable — certainly, however, the moment passed. Their desire for some sort of hitherto only dreamt of art-music unity and the circumstances which drove them apart says a great deal about modernism. Modern artists and musicians are often regarded as taking a perverse delight in chaos and fragmentation, but in this era and for these artists at least, there was an underlying hankering not for diversity but for a lost unity, one especially poignant in those shattered times.

The influence of both the futurist and the Dadaist movements on contemporary, popular and left-field music has been pervasive and persistent. There are just a couple of degrees of separation between futurist musical theorist Luigi Russolo and Frank Zappa — Edgard

Varèse is the link. Journalist Paul Morley's obsession with futurism prompted him to name the mid-'80s pop label he co-founded ZTT, after Filippo Marinetti's phonetic poem *Zang Tuum Tumb*, while Russolo's *Art of Noises* manifesto inspired the name of one of the label's principal groups.

As for Dadaism, the parallels between it and the punk movement have proven irresistible to some — its explosive iconoclasm, its insolence in the face of authority, its primal aesthetic revolt and its liberation of ideas from the stifling over-dominance of technique were echoed in punk, though there's not much proof that groups like The Damned and The Ramones were paying much conscious homage to the likes of Richard Huelsenbeck and Tristan Tzara when they first thrashed out a chord in anger. Cabaret Voltaire, the Sheffield electronic group, certainly were, while Brian Eno made direct reference to Kurt Schwitters's *Ur Sonata* on his *Kurt's Rejoinder*, with Talking Heads playing the same compliment to Hugo Ball on *I Zimbra*. Tiny allusions crop up here and there in contemporary culture — a writer/blogger naming herself Emmy Hennings after Hugo Ball's partner and fellow poet, for example. Far broader and less calculable, however, have been the influence of the Dadaists' experiments with chance, their extension of Picasso's innovations in collage and their paradoxical impulses — destruction and pacifism, anger and hilarity, nihilism and rebirth. What's strange, then, is while they provided useful rhetorical frameworks for modern music, they didn't actually produce a great deal of music themselves.

The futurist movement was formally and publicly inaugurated on the front page of *Le Figaro* in an astonishing publicity coup by their founder, Marinetti. It was the culmination of energies that had been gathering in the boiler rooms of the new industrial age for decades. Advertising hoardings blared from the sides of buildings while factory whistles, the revving and backfiring of steam and motor engines, the drone and hum of heavy machinery and the reverberation of telegraph wires were an increasing reality of everyday life, and worrying to some. The impressionists would occasionally include a distant factory in the background of their paintings, or acknowledge the jolly bustle of the music hall and the sodium glow of the gaslights, but artists preferred *nature morte*, the stoical rustic peasant peeling an apple, the lily pond, scenes of bucolic stillness, while in literature, the likes of Thomas Hardy, far from the madding crowd, looked out with justifiable fretfulness across the landscape and wondered what terrible new stormclouds were gathering over the new century's horizon.

Only the futurists embraced, with unbridled glee and gusto, what they correctly recognised as the transformation of mankind by his own mechanical creations. Emerging, blinking from a richness of mosque lamps, rugs and "domes of filigreed brass", the over-opulent trappings of the symbolist orientalism and art nouveau of his day, Marinetti recounts a fictional motor ride in which he purges the "mythology and the mystical ideal" of art's dead past. Having survived a spin into a ditch, Marinetti steps up, blackened but unbowed, brandishing his manifesto. Exalting aggressive action and a love of danger and war above the enfeebled and inert pensiveness of the traditional artist, Marinetti advocates a new dynamism which scorns conventional morality and consigns the sacred to the dustbin. "We affirm that the world's magnificence has been enriched by a new beauty; the beauty of speed. A racing car [...] a roaring car that seems to ride on grapeshot is more beautiful than the Victory of Samothrace." Pledging to "destroy all libraries and museums", Marinetti talks of "scorn for women" and the "utilitarian cowardice" of both moralism and feminism. These conspicuous signs of misogyny are telling, and they are of course grist to those who equate the futurist-inspired noise music of the late twentieth/early twenty-first century, such as the powernoise movement, with excessive machismo, or to those who detect an obnoxiously phallic dimension to industrial/economic expansion in general. But Marinetti's manifesto is anti-utopian in its radicalism and idealism. "Art," he declares, "can be nothing but violence, cruelty and injustice", a line that contains more than just perverse glee brought on by the intoxication of the petrol fumes in his nostrils.

Hereafter, the futurists embarked on a programme of events and manifestos designed to update all aspects of human life, a programme whose fascistic undertones have not gone unnoticed (Marinetti was an admirer of Mussolini). First and foremost there was futurist art, of course, whose most effective exponent was probably Umberto Boccioni, whose life was cut short by the World War Marinetti had so heartily welcomed. Influenced by cubism and perhaps Marcel Duchamp's use of "light as a mobile factor" in his painting *Nude Descending a Staircase*, it sought to introduce the principles of dynamism into the composition of painting, as if trying to emulate in the medium of oils some sort of cinematographic effect. Although Boccioni produced some fine works (his *Those Who Go* and *Those Who Stay* in particular, in which the contrasting moods of the adventurous departers and those they leave behind on the railway station are captured in the form, rather than the content of the pictures), it is hard to disagree with the expressionist Franc Marc, who wrote to Kandinsky that, although he found futurist ideas brilliant, he was "in no doubt whatsoever as to the mediocrity of their works". Nonetheless, scores of them still hang as permanent exhibits in London, Paris and New York.

The futurists further declared their intentions to transform the realms of theatre, architecture, the written word (no more syntax, decreed Marinetti — "imagination without strings" would be the new watchword), food (down with pasta), men's clothing and even lust, which would hereinafter be more futuristic in nature; almost a century on, these manifestos now read like a mix of the visionary and the risible. But it was Luigi Russolo's 1913 manifesto, *Art of Noises*, which has had the most far reaching effect down the decades.

For the first time since Psalm 98 exhorted the faithful to "make a joyful noise unto the Lord", Russolo admitted Noise in through the city gates of aesthetic acceptability, outside which it had roared in dissonant exile for centuries, its purpose then (and, for a great many people, now) to define that which was not musical. However, Russolo argued that noise, from the primal noises of nature to the mighty engines of modern industry, was not just a possible option but also central to the futurist imperative. "Ancient life was all silence," wrote Russolo. "With the invention of the machine, noise was born." He regarded the "complex polyphony" of nineteenth-century classical music as merely paving the way for the "creation of MUSICAL NOISE" which would be the signature of the twentieth. And, pertinently aware that among the most profound changes wrought in the modern age were in the soundscape, Russolo declared, "We find far more enjoyment in the combination of the noises of trams, backfiring motors, carriages and bawling crowds than in rehearing, for example, the 'Eroica' or the 'Pastoral'." Expressing dissatisfaction with the paltry results yielded by orchestral players sawing with futility at such passéist stringed instruments as the violin, Russolo called for the construction of instruments which would introduce a whole new range of tones into the realm of organised sound, reflecting in their irregularity the irregularity of modern life. These would generate six new "families of noises" which Russolo set out, including rumbles, roars, crashes, booms, whistles, screeches, shouts, screams and groans.

To this end, Russolo actually set about building his famous Noise Intoners, which were the subject of much newspaper coverage and inevitable, gleefully coruscating remarks about the sounds that emanated therefrom. These prototype synthesisers were certainly cumbersome devices — solid boxes with huge metal speakers, operated by levers. They came under four categories: Exploders, Cracklers, Buzzers and Scrapers. In April 1914, the wealthy and well-connected Marinetti arranged a private concert at his home at which the "Sound Intonators" would be unveiled and demonstrated. Among those present were impresario Sergio Diaghlev and a young Igor Stravinsky. The composer was reportedly enthralled by the Crackler in particular; leaping off his divan in response to the shower of noises it generated, he bounded to his piano in a vain effort to find some equivalent on the range of that instrument. The demonstration was well received, and the Intoners went out on the road. They went to London, where after the reviewer from the *Times* expressed his bewilderment and the initial public reaction was one of mockery, the Intoners were again warmly received. Marinetti was gratified by this, although as a provocateur, he would equally have cherished a negative response. In Italy, by contrast, a performance of the Intoners, their operators in full evening dress, was disrupted and culminated in Russolo punching a defamatory journalist from the newspaper *L'Italia* in the eye, for which he landed up in court. Marinetti sneered that demonstrating the noise Intoners to the Italian public had been "like showing the first steam engine to a herd of cows". Though any competent history of modern and electronic music assigns the Noise Intoners their proper place, they weren't widely adopted. In fact, Italian Casavola was the only notable composer to use them. Russolo's original models disappeared; one was supposedly destroyed in 1930, at a Paris screening of *L'Age d'Or*, where an audience, enraged at the film's anti-Catholic content, smashed it to pieces while it was exhibited in the foyer. The Intoners weren't capable of bearing out the radical implications of Russolo's *Art of Noises* manifesto, and, despite the initial shock and intrigue they generated, it would soon have become clear that in themselves they were glorified, oversized music boxes, cranking out risible threeps and chirps which hardly did justice to the rhetorical blare that had given birth to them. Ezra Pound's dismissive description of the machines as the "mimetic representation of dead cats in a foghorn" may not have been wide of the mark. The real noise generated by the futurists was the howls of outrage at their deliberately confrontational and audience-participatory Variety Theatre, in which Marinetti's exercises in "words in freedom" were coupled with cacophonous instrumental accompaniments, all designed to mock to the ground the cherished relics of traditional culture and festival customs. In 1914, in a gallery in Rome, a group of futurists produced a clamorous racket on violins, drums, saws and bells while the artist Balla emerged leading a procession of actors wearing black tubes with holes punched in them for eyes, as Marinetti delivered a funeral oration for a "passéist" critic struck down by futurism.

Although such events often descended, inevitably, into chaos (with perhaps those who turned up fully aware that all this was part of the evening's entertainment, armed in advance with rotten fruit), it's also worth noting that a respectfulness for that which declared itself art, and moreover professed to be the latest thing, was enough to cow some audiences, particularly in London, into passive appreciativeness. Indeed, at one performance at London's Doré Gallery in 1914, a futurist rendering of the Siege of Adrianople, in which the divisions between performers and audience were deliberately assailed by the dynamic stage setting, nonetheless failed to engender the audience participation Marinetti was hoping for. "This has been a very incomplete performance," he boomed in frustration at the onlookers, for whom the sacrosanctness of the art gallery had proven inviolable.

Running in parallel to Italian futurism was the Russian futurist movement, more complex in its relationship with the natural world, which it did not hold in the same scorn as their Italian counterparts, for whom it represented the passéist, placid silence of the dead past, which backfiring motor engines and factory sirens had come to displace. Russia was, after all, an overwhelmingly peasant-based population and the cubo-futurist works of Kazimir Malevich draw upon the colours and earth tones of the pre-industrial world in which they dwelt. That said, they understood that the onset of mechanisation was at hand, while the imminent seismic event for them was the Revolution.

This sense of impending mechanisation was reflected in the "man-machine" aesthetic of 1913's *Victory over the Sun*, billed as the "world's first futurist opera", a veritable Gesamtkunstwerk in which poet and playwright Aleksei Kruchenykh and composer and art theoretician Mikhail Matiushin collaborated with Kazimir Malevich, who designed sets and costumes in which the actors, according to Kruchenykh, "resembled machines in motion" in their wire and cardboard outfits — precursors of Kraftwerk's man-machines. Matiushin's soundtrack, meanwhile, dispensed with conventional structures in favour of dissonance, quarter tones with sound-colour correspondence, the dream of Scriabin, worked into his musical score.

The Russian futurists did share the Italians' contempt for their grand cultural heritage, which they suggested was about to be felled like great oaks to make way for the paving of the new age, or, as they put it in a 1912 manifesto, *A Slap in the Face of Public Taste:* "Toss Pushkin, Dostoevsky, Tolstoy and so on from the steamship of modernity." But their excitement, their impetus, came from the coming Revolution, whose date the poet Mayakovsky accurately foretold, rather than the quasi-fascistic pipe dreams of the Italians.

The too-brief tale of the alliance between Russian avant-garde art and the Soviet state is a sad and familiar one, littered with abandoned monuments such as Tatlin's *Tower* or *Monument to the Third International* (1919–20), a huge, helter skelter-like edifice which would have stood far taller than the Eiffel Tower, pointing with diagonal intent into the future. There is some doubt as to whether it would have actually stood up had they attempted to erect it, a doubt that extends to whether the relationship between experimental Russian art and the Soviet leadership would have endured even if there had been no Stalin, no imposition of socialist realism. Great as works such as El Lissitzky's *Beat the Whites with the Red Wedge*, for example, are, they were conditional on unqualified support for the regime rather than truly free creative expressions. This was the case from pretty much 1917 onwards. For how long would this have been tolerable?

The great surge of activity during the Russian futurist years, pre- and post-1917, is formidable; much of the art is preserved, including a cache of some 40,000 artworks accumulated in Uzbekistan by the Russian artist and collector Igor Savitsky, from 1931 onwards, housed since 1966 in the Nukus Museum of Art on the western fringes of the country, an institution later imperilled by the rise of the Uzbek nationalist President Islam Karimov. There were numerous efforts also to create a prototype electronic music, though that which has survived is scratchy or notional at best.

There does remain one great sound monument to the Russian futurist era, however. In 1922, the composer Arseny Avraamov, a conscientious objector in World War I, who fled Russia only to return after the Revolution, put together his *Symphony of Factory Sirens* to mark the fifth anniversary of the Soviet state. It involves a mass band and choir, navy ship sirens, whistles, bus and car horns, factory sirens, cannons, the foghorns of the Soviet flotilla in the Caspian Sea, artillery guns, machine guns and hydro-airplanes, and was conducted by a team using flags and pistols to co-ordinate the sequenced bursts of sound activity, performed across the city of Baku.

In 2003, the work was recreated by Leopoldo Amigo and Miguel Molina under the title *Baku: Symphony of Sirens*. The reconstruction of the piece manages to convey the sense of immense space between the sound sources; explosive, exclamatory, triumphant, it is Eisensteinian in both its ingenuity and its misplaced faith in the Soviet state, given what was just around the corner in 1922. Machine-generated and involving the juxtaposition of industrial sounds that are non-musical in origin, it is a magnificent prototype for the great electronic works which would be produced decades later.

The futurists' attempts at what they grandly dubbed "Dynamic and Synoptic Declamation", which in its most extreme forms meant a full-scale riot, were the precursor of similar events staged by the Dadaists. However, that movement began unassumingly, in the form of a "literary cabaret", entitled the Cabaret Voltaire, in an upstairs room at a bar in Niederdorf, a seedy quarter of Zurich, in 1916 (this was the same city and year in which Lenin was rather less noisily plotting the Russian Revolution). A typical evening might see patrons munching sandwiches and drinking beer while Emmy Hennings delivers chansons in a rather shrill and reedy voice, and balalaika orchestras play recitals of works by traditional German, Russian and Swiss poets. However, there were also piano renderings of the music of the French composer Saint-Saens, as well as exhibitions of paintings by Robert Delaunay. Before long, however, the more Bruitist elements already practised by futurism would invade the Cabaret Voltaire soirées. Tristan Tzara accompanied his poems with cowbells and sharp, rhythmical accompaniment on tables and boxes, while the Berlin Dadaist and doctor Richard Huelsenbeck played out his role as Dada Drummer, reciting his own semi-phonetic poetry over tom-toms playing "negro rhythms", which were now invading literature in the way African masks had "disfigured" Picasso's *Les Demoiselles D'Avignon*, at the moment at which modernity in art was effectively birthed.

It is probably just as well that there was no way of recording some of these performances, if only because the Dadaists' dalliances with negritude, in all its exotic otherness, would seem naive, even inadvertently racist, to modern eyes and ears. What's clear is that, while Dada's contributions to literature and the visual arts are tangible and still graphically impressive, the noises they made, uncapturable in the silent era and probably designed with little more purpose than to clear the stuffy cultural air of the time, are negligible by comparison. Schoenberg pieces were occasionally played at Dada events, but Schoenberg himself regarded the Dadaists as faddists and saw no crossover between his own work, which only sought to "destroy" the great classical tradition in order to save it, and the anarchistic antics of the Zurich hell raisers. Erik Satie, author of *Memoirs of an Amnesiac*, the man who claimed to be the only Frenchman to understand English humour (thanks to his part-Scottish parentage), receives honorary membership in the Dada annals. However, apart from *Vexations*, a precursor of the sound installations of the late twentieth century, designed to be played for 28 hours on a continuing cycle, and *Parade*, his ballet which featured various noise-making instruments such as typewriter and foghorn, Satie is generally famous for his neoclassical style, jaunty and limpid by turns, which, like his dapper appearance, functions as a deceptively well-turned-out front for his more mischievous and absurdist intentions.

Hans Arp sums up the utopian spirit which fired the Dadaists into action against the distant backdrop of the cannon's roar, and which urged them to take up the radical means that they did. In

Dadaland, he wrote, "Revolted by the butchery of the 1914 World War, we in Zurich devoted ourselves to the arts. While the guns rumbled in the distance, we sang, painted, made collages and wrote poems with all our might. We were seeking an art based on fundamentals, to cure the madness of the age, and a new order of things that would restore the balance between heaven and hell. We had a dim premonition that power-mad gangsters would one day use art itself as a means of deadening men's minds." There are those for whom that premonition would cruelly resonate in the modern day, in a world dominated by corporations which, far from being scandalised by abstract art, has assimilated it and even promotes it as a means of self-validation. In themselves, the Dadaists were not principally innovators — their experiments with chance and its role in delving into the unconscious were new, and led directly to surrealism, but their extensive use of cubist and collage techniques, as well as their phonetic poetry, owe clear debts to the cubists and futurists respectively. What was new, and why they remain such vibrant precursors of contemporary musicians, was their strong, countercultural impulse. As a matter of conscience rather than merely a desire to make trouble, they wanted to break down the divides between art and life, jolt the "masses" out of their torpor and storm the hermetic citadels of those who regarded art as a refuge from the everyday. Dada made its anti-message felt in the theatre, in cinema (via the short films of Hans Richter and Viking Eggeling), in Hans Arp's plaintively affirmative abstract works, in Kurt Schwitters's cherishing of a discarded bus ticket as part of his working palette, in the surly pranks of Georg Grosz, in the tentative and short-lived venture into leftist politics by Richard Huelsenbeck at the end of World War I when Berlin was briefly up for grabs, in the debauched poet Arthur Cravan fighting the black American heavyweight Jack Johnson for a single round, in the public outrages perpetrated by Johannes Baader (who once interrupted a service at Berlin Cathedral by crying out "To hell with Christ!") and, of course, in Marcel Duchamp's urinal exhibited with the signature "R. Mutt"; all of these could be claimed as Dadaist manifestations.

Dada prefigured abstract art, surrealist art, outsider art, conceptual art. In that respect, it has succeeded. In its efforts to bring about a radical transformation in human consciousness, its success is rather more debatable. The "power-mad gangsters" feel more powerful than ever, while R. Mutt's urinal is pored over in the Tate, as viewers cast their eye respectfully over its porcelain contours and bathe in its sacred do-not-touchness, despite Duchamp's intentions. (I recently saw one student set down in front of the exhibit, earnestly sketching the thing. Why?) If the Dadaist spirit persists, it is spotted here and there, for example in the anti-works of renegades from the rock world, particularly the KLF, whose merciless pursuit of Rachel Whiteread and burning of a million pounds weren't just clever happenings in the old Dadaist tradition but struck surgically at the malfunctioning heart of the prevailing, complacent attitudes of the art world. Dada fed music in all kinds of ways except with music itself. In this respect it was as silent as the era.

There was, however, one composer who found a way of incorporating into his work the levelling trumpet-blasts of the great art movements of the early twentieth century. Edgard Varèse had been sufficiently impressed by Russolo's "Russolophone" constructed in 1929, to display it in Paris, albeit to little enthusiasm. As a starving youth estranged from the family home after a mildly Oedipal altercation, having beaten up his father when he tried to strike his mother, Varèse visited Picasso's studio in Paris and, as the artist tucked into his own supper, was too awestruck to ask him if he might spare a bite to eat. He contributed to the Dadaist periodical *391* — though he himself did not regard his music as "Dadaist", being out of sympathy with their anti-art manifesto. To Varèse, art was what redeemed life. And, while agreeing with the futurists that the new century would require new and mechanical modes of expression, he deplored their obsession with the material trappings of modern life — omnibuses, newspaper headlines, etc., which he regarded as "superficial and boring". He did not go into raptures of epiphany whenever he heard an exhaust pipe backfire. His music, he said, was determined by the "exigencies of my inner rhythm" — which is what makes it more rich and transcendent than the concertos for factory sirens written by others he is associated with, but which he considered merely "imitative" as opposed to creative.

Varèse was probably the first composer to talk about music in terms of "organised sound", which germinated in his mind at the turn of the century following an encounter with the writings of the physicist, musicologist and philosopher Hoene-Wroński, who defined music as "the corporealisation of the intelligence that is in sounds". With a protean temperament which seemed to have sent even his hair into a state of shock, Varèse had no time for the traditional classical canon. He professed to find Mozart "boring" and, itching with futurist fervour, he quit his studies at the Paris Conservatoire and fell under the thrall of contemporary composers such as Debussy and Busoni. He spent much of his working life chafing at the limits of traditional instruments, which, he wrote, "Had conditioned our ears to accept only an infinitesimal part of the infinite sounds in nature." Clearly, he was anticipating electronic instruments, but when he saw prototypes like Dr Thaddeus Cahill's Dynamophone demonstrated, he was disappointed. Varèse duly did what he could within the constraints of the orchestral lexicon, importing from Dada and futurism the notions of Bruitism and simultaneism, and realising them in sound.

In 1915, Varèse fatefully set sail for New York, after having been invalided out of the French Army and encountering difficulties in making ends meet in his home country. As with Marcel Duchamp, his move across the Atlantic anticipated a later, fundamental shift in modern art's centre of gravity from Europe to America. In halting English, he explained to an American reporter that he was looking for "mechanical mediums which will lend themselves to every expression of thought and keep up with thought". Sadly, this was to be a lifelong search.

Although he was accepted politely into New York society and attained a position as a conductor, the musical establishment blanched at his modernity and the New Symphony Orchestra he formed was disbanded when he refused to appease audiences and sponsors by not even lobbing them a conciliatory bone of Beethoven in his ultra-modernist repertoire. Despite the mixed reaction he received in America (in 1924, Olin Downes compared his composition *Hyperprism* to the "noise of a factory accident"), Varèse assimilated the twentieth-century Manhattan experience into the fibres of his work. His apartment was close enough to the Hudson River for him to hear the noises and foghorns drifting through his windows, coupled with what he described as the "parabolas and hyperbolas" of the passing fire engines. In 1921, he composed *Amériques.* Despite its relative brevity, at just under 25 minutes, it feels vast in its orchestral range — 27 woodwind and 29 brass instruments are employed. Its use of noise-making devices is superficially reminiscent of the futurists sirens — it deploys steamboat whistles, cyclone whistles and crow calls, "sound masses" which ghost through the piece, as well as a formidable battery of percussion — and one might accuse Varèse of showing the "imitative" tendencies he decried in the futurists. But there is more to *Amériques* than that. It's a veritable New York 25 minutes, with "sound masses" coming at you every which way like cross-town traffic, and rhythmically girded bodies of orchestral noise erupting and towering like instantaneously erected skyscrapers. It can be taken as a tone poem to the United States, formidably urbane but laced with the occasional, wistful phrase that hankers after the Old Country. Structurally and thematically, however, it goes beyond that. "With *Amériques*, I began to write my own music," says Varèse, and you might say that it represents a point at which classical music is hoist upright, from the horizontal to the vertical, with a new stress on rhythm, timbre and noise/colour, in keeping with the new eruption of inner energies which would fill in the twentieth century. The title of the piece, with its plural, is apposite in translation — the "Americas", land of multiple possibilities and outcomes. The past is singular but the future is plural.

However, Varèse's dreams were deferred. *Amériques* wasn't performed for five years. In 1928, he returned briefly to Paris to rework *Amériques* to include parts for the recently developed ondes Martenot. However, such inventions only went a little way in helping him achieve his visions for "organised sound". In 1931, he composed *Ionisation*, the first classical piece to be written entirely for percussive instruments. With its unique combination of noises and glissandi scales, it's like the sound of a man hammering at the unopened door of tomorrow. Around this time, he proposed and drew up plans for a "musical laboratory", the like of which would not exist in reality until the introduction of magnetic tape. Varèse was 20 years too soon. Meanwhile, the critics viewed his work with, at best, the polite but uncomprehending deference of the fashion-conscious, and at worst, open hostility. In 1932, one Berlin critic snarled that Varèse's supremely rational, meticulously organised *Arcana* was "insane and barbarous".

During the 1920s and 1930s, developments in classical music were steady and incremental. Shostakovitch and Prokofiev forged links as best they could between tradition and modernity but always under the watchful gaze of the Communist Party, who blew hot and cold with them, according to their "deviancies". Bartók and Kodály re-energised and lent a new angularity to their music by incorporating elements of Hungarian folk. The Second Viennese School, Schoenberg and his pupils Webern and (before his untimely death) Berg developed the principles of "twelve tone" composition, with Webern in particular developing a minimal, delicately but devastatingly precise, spatially conscious, near-evanescent compositional style which at times hovered on the threshold of silence and speaks of a terrifying existential solitude which runs like a chill through much of twentieth-century music, Miles Davis included. All of this, however, took place against the uninhibited, transatlantic roar of the Jazz Age (Dvorak had predicted decades earlier that Black Americans would supply the musical idiom of the twentieth century) and, while not paling in comparison, struggled to match it on the new century's terms of volume, temperature and community excitement. Composers such as Stravinsky and particularly Darius Milhaud of the Group des Six did attempt to enliven their work by taking on board jazz elements, with some success. Duke Ellington, meanwhile, was emerging as the first great jazz composer, and facing the same accusations of "dissonance" as his classical contemporaries. ("We live in dissonant times," he suavely retorted).

Meanwhile, modern art was dominated on the one hand by the Bauhaus movement and the East European constructivist movement, who more rigidly formalised the ideas of Kandinsky and the expressionists, using precise, rectilinear forms. An artist like Mondrian was initially under the spell of cubism but developed his own systems, frustrated that cubism didn't make the final push beyond guitars, bowls of fruit and the like, into the abstract, "an expression of pure reality", depicting visually the "spiritual realm". Artists such as El Lissitzky cheerfully volunteered for propaganda work; *Beat the Whites with the Red Wedge* expresses, in constructivist terms, a desire for victory against the reactionary corps of the Russian White Army, while Kazimir Malevich, pioneer of Dynamic Suprematism, put his work at the service of the Soviets in the Tenth State Exhibition of 1919, with the clear implication that Suprematism in art was a corollary of the supremacy of communism. Of course, it wasn't long before Stalin did an abrupt volte-face, relieved the avant-garde of their duties as State Artists and supplanted them with the banal, figurative friezes of socialist realism.

Although Bauhaus renegade Paul Klee looked for connections between music and art in his own work, speaking of its "polyphonic" nature, contemporary music didn't really have the wherewithal to match these developments in the art world. Perhaps one could make a case for Webern, but although his work was condemned as "cultural Bolshevism" by the Nazis, Webern was hardly of the Malevich stripe — in 1940, he expressed admiration for Hitler, and ended his days in an internment camp, accidentally shot dead by an American soldier in 1945 as he stepped out for a cigarette.

The pre-war period was dominated on the other hand by the surrealist movement. Although the name was coined by Apollinaire, the movement's leader was a young ex-Dadaist, André Breton. A student of Freud, who had applied his techniques to shell-shocked troops hospitalised in World War I, Breton appears on the face of it to have been an extraordinary ill-suited figure to spearhead a movement based on free association, free thought, uninhibited exploration of the unconscious and artistic techniques designed to stir its repressed energies. He was a humourless prig, a misogynist who actively demoralised his wife when she attempted to forge an artistic career of her own. He was a homophobe, despite the feelings of longing and infatuation he nourished for one Jacques Vaché, his war comrade who died in 1919, coining the disgusted phrase "promotion of homosexuality" decades in advance of the British Conservative Party. He was an autocrat who brooked little dissent, facets which were exposed for posterity to his disadvantage when he tried to face down Salvador Dalí in a "show trial" brought against the artist for showing insufficient enthusiasm for the Communist party. And yet, he somehow corralled and in many cases cowed the leading artists of his age into the surrealist movement, including figures as diverse as the ex-Dadaist Tristan Tzara, Rene Magritte, Marcel Duchamp, Pablo Picasso, Louis Aragon, Yves Tanguy as well as Dalí himself, exercising a powerful charm over them and ensuring that what otherwise have been a disparate set of careers and bodies of work coalesced into a very definite art movement whose grip on the public imagination remains stronger than that of any other in the twentieth century, and whose central term, "surreal", is the most embedded in everyday language. Perhaps it was Breton's asceticism which inspired and shamed his artist followers and led them, like so many disciples, to take up his injunction to "set out on the road" in the first surrealist manifesto. Although he was often in a desperate state of penury, he adamantly refused to sell the many original works of art he owned, a sternly idealistic gesture of anti-capitalism which serves as a burning, reproachful example to the present day.

Salvador Dalí, of course, had no such qualms; André Breton created the anagram Avida Dollars for him. Indeed, Dalí worked his love of money into his aesthetic — for him it was a proud precept rather than a weakness. As a true surrealist, Dalí felt he should no more suppress his avarice than he should his desire to take a shit, or indeed, his erotic admiration of Adolf Hitler. Dalí went to America and conquered the young country, conceiving and creating an enduring parody of the Great Modern European Artist, with his swivelling eyes, twirling moustaches, exaggerated outrageously foreign accent and, of course, his soft watches. He appeared on the cover of *Time* magazine in 1937, wrote a screenplay for Harpo Marx, and was guest of honour at "surrealist banquets", including one at which all the food served was dyed blue, doted over by wide-eyed wealthy American widows, whose patronage of the arts remains a staple to this day. Dalí was the first modern artist unselfconsciously to court glamour and celebrity, lending the visual arts a prestige and curiosity that has paid dividends ever since — shamelessly, he more or less did as he pleased, from doing TV adverts for chocolate to (at the end of his life) attaching his signature to blank scrolls of paper whose contents would be filled in later by some other person. He got away with it, because as a deep-dyed surrealist, all of his actions, however dubious or unscrupulous, were therefore spontaneously "surrealist" also.

In Hollywood, in 1937, Salvador Dalí met George Antheil, the composer of *Ballet Mécanique*, who was stationed out there. He greeted him effusively, dubbing him "the greatest Surrealist on earth." However, while surrealism lent itself perfectly to imagistic and representational genres — the cinema (Bunuel's *L'Age d'Or* and *Un Chien Andalou*), literature and, of course, the visual arts, there was no "surrealist music" to speak of — at least, prior to World War II. Breton was eventually an admirer of John Cage and, inevitably, *4'33"*, though, ironically, that is a piece about the impotence and absence of music; he believed that music could reach further into the unconscious than any other art form, since it was inherently non-representational and therefore less constrained by social, political and cultural "meaning". However, in his manifestos, the essential surrealist texts, Breton pays very little attention to music at all. Perhaps Breton, a literary man, needed the footholds of the "constraints" of his own form more than he let on. World War II would inevitably cleave a profound schism across the history of twentieth-century art. It's intriguing that the Nazis should have taken the trouble to decry, and sarcastically exhibit, what they termed Degenerate Art, which is to say, that which was infected by "Jewish" values — twisted, ugly, depraved, and deviant. For Hitler, Jewishness and modernity were synonymous, even though only six of the 112 artists exhibited at the Degenerate Art exhibition of 1937 were actually Jewish. The exhibition was to be contrasted with one of more wholesome, Aryan, blood and soil, art of the sort favoured by the Führer. (While two million people witnessed the Degenerate Art exhibition, only four hundred thousand turned up to look at the officially sanctioned works.) The "degenerate" artists displayed included Otto Dix, Georg Grosz, Max Ernst, Max Pechstein, Hans Richter, Kurt Schwitters and Franz Marc.

There was also a "Degenerate Music" exhibition. The cover to the guide for this depicted a grotesque figment of the Nazis' hateful delusions — a huge-lipped, virtually simian black man with an earring, honking into a saxophone and sporting a conspicuous Star of David rosette on his lapel. The music of Schoenberg was sneeringly exhibited; atonal music was banned in Germany, as was jazz or "jazz-tinged" classical music, such as that of the relatively innocuous Hindemith. All of this was considered "politically unlistenable", in contrast to Wagner, hailed as a paradigm of "anti-Semitic" music and the Nazi composer Hans Pfitzner, who preached against the jeopardy into which civilisation was plunged by twelve tone composition and the "alien" genre of jazz.

Modern art and modern music were, therefore, in the same boat when it came to Nazi antipathy. However, it is not quite that simple. The German scholar Georg Bassmann has argued that there was no inherent need for the Nazis to shun modern art, and, had they commandeered it for their own purposes, they could have built a bridge with the "liberal educated middle class". Indeed, at the time, the German Art Society's management committee told the Nazis,

"We beg to be of service". In much the same way as intellectuals like Martin Heidegger were co-opted by the Nazis, so, Bassmann argues, could a great many modern artists have been and added a potent, modernistic, visual component to Nazi propaganda — for a while, at any rate. And, after all, the red, white and black of the swastika flag is nothing if not a starkly effective abstract image, bold and direct in its geometry and use of colour. Hitler, however, was an artist himself and therefore not disinterested enough to have made such a decision. Moreover, he was perhaps at some level aesthetically conscious that the content of expressionist art in particular, or the brutal, insolent satire of Georg Grosz, told deeper truths about the noble German people than he could bear to witness.

What, however, of "degenerate" music? Could it, too, have been similarly co-opted? Jazz, of course, was out of the question from a racial point of view, and all of the classical work whose white waters it had poisoned. As has been noted, Webern, with astonishing naivety, did express admiration for Hitler. Yet, even if he had offered up his services to the Nazi cause, it's hard to see how he would have been taken up. His *Vier Lieder Opus 13* was no match, in the great march forward, for the gravel-scrunching simplicity of the *Horst Wessel Lied*. This, then, was one of the salvations of the music of the avant-garde — it could not be co-opted. It was, indeed remains, useless, in the most sublimely useful sense of that word.

CHAPTER 3

STOCKHAUSEN, FLUXUS AND ALL THAT JAZZ

The years following World War II were a time of sudden, rapid and astonishing development. In the sound laboratories of Germany and France, Pierre Schaeffer and Herbert Eimert were laying the foundations for musique concrète and electronic music, respectively.

Alongside his indispensable assistant, Pierre Henry, with whom he co-founded the Groupe de Recherche Musicales (GRM), Schaeffer worked with what Michel Chion described as a "desperate rationalism" to develop the new index of possibilities that had been brought about with the invention of magnetic tape — he was presented with his first tape recorder in 1951. Now, at last, collage, which Picasso had introduced into the fabric of modern art almost 40 years earlier, was to be a working component of music. John Cage had prefigured this back in 1939, with his prescient work for turntables, as had Schaeffer himself at the Office de Radiodiffusion Télévision Française. However, with magnetic tape, it was now theoretically possible, in the realms of sound, to make anything out of anything. The scope for raw materials was now infinite, and the options as to how you worked on that material, with the studio now as much an editing suite as a place where music was merely recorded, were greatly expanded. "We have at our disposal the generality of sounds", wrote Schaeffer, "at least in principle, without having to produce them. All we have to do is push the button on a tape recorder." Sounds could be wrenched from their original context, looped, sped up, repeated, slowed down, juxtaposed, faded and overlaid. The opening "Ahoy!" of *Symphonie pour un Homme Seul* is a ghostly clarion call from a future past, a megaphone blast into the ear trumpet of hidebound musical conventions. Although much of Schaeffer's work is the diced and reassembled product of conventional instruments, he extracts from these sounds unearthly and disembodied qualities, and weaving them together with spools and scissors, he creates dreamlike, disorienting compositional tapestries in which the familiar is rendered only semi-familiar. They are as exciting and frightening as the times; technology continues apace but has created a world in which man, for the moment at least, has lost his bearings. In a work like *Orphée 53*, the sense of descent is palpable, the phrase "Paradis" quickening like a pulse, then decelerating, declining, into the underworld.

Meanwhile, in Cologne, in 1951, Herbert Eimert had persuaded his employers at Cologne Radio to create a studio specialising in electronic music. This would be the centre for a whole generation of composers, including Karlheinz Stockhausen, Iannis Xenakis and Henri Pousseur. Eimert was a controversial figure in the field of musicology, who had already written about serial music, which he believed not to be the "invention" of Arnold Schoenberg but something that was already in the compositional air. A fierce believer that music should be an exact science, a logical rather than natural process, he played down the role of the composer and what he believed to be the exaggerated role of personal psychology and expressionism in music, laying stress instead on the composition itself and the way in which it was received.

A quarrel at once erupted between the French pioneers in musique concrète, music made from "natural" sounds, and the

Cologne composers, who, by contrast, played "pure" electronic music, the equivalent of the oils in a palette rather than clipped-up bits of newspaper or similar "found items". Indeed, the composer Meyer-Eppler believed that, with electronic music, the composer would be similar to a visual artist, in that he would compose directly to tape, with the results then laid before the general public, like an artist exhibiting his canvasses, without the need for the mediation of conductor or composer. The same, of course, could be said of Schaeffer and co — however, there was a belief in Cologne that electronically generated music represented the more "authentic" and higher-quality option. They regarded themselves as in the hermetic tradition of serialism, taking their cue from Webern, and looking towards making a "total" serial music, now that electronics had reduced to atoms the former limits of interval and tone imposed by traditional orchestration.

The writer MJ Grant cites a novel by Herman Hesse, *The Glass Bead Game*, as exerting a profound influence over the serialist/ electronic composers, particularly Stockhausen. It speaks of a community who dedicate themselves to the pursuit of the title, in which the highest development of the human spirit is supposedly manifested. However, this life of pure meditation requires a complete detachment from the outside world. In the wake of World War II, Stockhausen was very taken with the cleansing and redeeming effects that could come from some "new spiritual order", and this reportedly impelled him to abandon his earlier, literary ambitions in favour of music. The attainment of some pure absolute appeared, for a while, to be within the grasp of electronic music, and seemed to be an attractive model for a way of living — a rational idealism, buffered from the fallen state of everyday reality, untroubled by expressionist, emotional trauma. However, it didn't take long for this stand-off between the advocates of a music based on a higher purity and one based on the "fallen" everyday to let up. Stockhausen realised by the early '50s that in the fallible context of everyday human existence, absolute ideals would always remain beyond reach, or would be soiled the moment you laid hands on them. By the mid-'50s, in works like *Gesang der Jünglinge*, he was making his own forays into musique concrète. As for Pierre Schaeffer, in later life he, too, relented and worked with electronically generated sounds. The quarrel, such as it was, seems a little quaint now, conducted in the embers of post-war Franco-German enmity. However, it indicated the logical utopianism in which, despite the depths to which humanity had just sunk, ideas about music making and its role in human existence were couched by its most "extreme" practitioners, fundamental ideas about man and matter. They didn't make this music out of sheer, maniacal wantonness, or to prod a stick in the midriff of bourgeois convention, to manufacture outrage, or simply to create novelty for novelty's sake. The studio pioneers in Cologne and Paris were conscientiously and meticulously laying the foundations for what today constitutes the vast majority of modern music, mainstream or otherwise, pop or academic, from Kylie Minogue to Can, from Ricardo Villalobos to the Mnemonists, from Kraftwerk to hip-hop auteurs like Jay Dee aka J Dilla. They weren't merely "paving the way", however — though some of their works have the feel of blueprint about them, others are masterpieces in their own right, more than just mere statements about the processes by which they were made and the forms they took. This was the dawn of music's own nuclear age, momentous and deserving of awe.

And nobody cared.

I use the word "nobody" in its demographic, rather than literal sense, of course. However, all this cultural investigation and innovation had the misfortune to be taking place in ruined, discredited, old Europe. The locus of modern culture, meanwhile, had shifted to the United States. As we have already seen, the likes of Varèse and Marcel Duchamp had long since made the transatlantic shift, while Dalí had already seduced Hollywood. However, the artistic flight from Europe now saw the likes of Max Ernst and André Breton lead a whole raft of artists and thinkers whose lives were endangered by the Nazis and their concomitant hatred of "degenerate" art. Not everybody made it — Robert Desnos, for example, died in a concentration camp, while there was a modicum of traffic in the other direction — the American photographer and surrealist Man Ray, for example, settled permanently in Paris after the war. However, those who made the boat trip to New York and had a taste of Manhattan and the patronage of the Guggenheims and their like showed no immediate inclination to return to Europe — especially because it turned out that Paris showed no general civic inclination to welcome back its artistic sons and daughters from American exile.

It turned out that the city was a great deal more bourgeois and conservative, a good deal less gay, than had generally been supposed — it seemed it had played host only with great reluctance to the great art movements of the pre-war era.

Whereas the war had taken a terrible economic toll in Europe, America had emerged from it with its position as an economic superpower greatly strengthened. Manhattan in particular would add to the country's general spoils a newfound status as the world capital of modern culture. Jazz, meanwhile, was continuing its rapid, evolutionary arc with the innovations of Charlie Parker, Dizzy Gillespie and the bebop generation. Figures like Duke Ellington and Louis Armstrong were now household names, despite lingering racial antipathy. Meanwhile, rock and roll, fermenting on the peripheries of rhythm and blues, was about to explode into being — the irresistible upshot of youth's growing sense of its own freedom, identity and spending capacity. In the words of Billy Wilder, the rise of TV gave something cinema to look down on but was an increasing part of the everyday cultural wallpaper. America was unleashing the inner energies pre-echoed by Varèse — the smartest, dumbest country in the world, the most exquisitely metropolitan and crudely reactionary, the place to be, unless they didn't happen to like your kind, and even then, still, maybe, the place to be. (There was, of course, a post-war jazz exodus from America to Europe, a flight from domestic racism, but only a few really stuck it — most of the major jazz players remained in America.) It was in this broad, quotidian context in which the likes of Schaeffer and Stockhausen toiled. No headlines in *Le Figaro* for them, no place in the cultural timeline — rather, they stood on the edge of an ever-widening gulf between the musical avant-garde and the material everyday, on the margins of an altogether new media environment.

It was in this context, also, that abstract expressionism, the first great movement of the second half of the twentieth century, thrived, and Jackson Pollock came to the fore. Though it would be an exaggeration to suggest that his works were greeted with total and instantaneous comprehension by the general public, at the same time he was not marginalised — indeed, he became a celebrity of sorts when, in 1949, he was profiled by *Life* magazine. He lent himself to that magazine's visual brief both as an artist and a would-be icon. His manly, laconic air was distinctly all-American. Beret-less and lacking in the flouncy, extravagant manners of the European artist-caricature, he came across not as a theoretician but as a strong and silent creature of pure artistic impulse, as lived up to in Ed Harris's depiction of him in *Pollock*, the film based on the artist's life. Pollock the artist is, of course, deserving of the lavish curiosity and tolerance conferred on his work, in which the viewer is invited to discern deeper patterns of meaning and expression beneath the apparent random and untutored chaos of its surfaces. Pollock the icon, perversely, benefits not just from his hard drinking but also from his death in an automobile accident at around the same time that James Dean died in similar circumstances, as if both were speeding along the same, fateful fast lane of modernity, leaving a fiery exhaust trail in their wake.

Charlie Parker, too, died in 1955, aged just 34 but with a lifetime of enormous appetites for all the good and bad things in life, bearing the broken body of an elderly, dissipated man. Parker was conscious of the works of Stravinsky and Edgard Varèse, both of whom were based in America during his lifetime, and both of whom he attempted to approach, the latter in the capacity of a pupil. Parker was a victim of the excesses of jazz's "street" life, who sadly inspired a raft of younger musicians not just in the digital intricacies of bebop but in the supposed artistic benefits of heroin ("to play like Bird, you gotta do like Bird," ran the depressing refrain). However, he also represents the point at which jazz makes the transition from the music of the street and the clubs, the feeder of popular music's watered down lexicon, into the academies. Parker was depressed both by the rise of rock and roll, its musical conservatism ("I got no kick against modern jazz — unless they try to play it too darn fast," went Chuck Berry's immortal lyric) and the fact that so many of his straitened bebop contemporaries gave up their more serious pursuits in order to take their places in their shiny jackets in the back line of rhythm and blues bands.

After Parker came The Modern Jazz Quartet, whose impeccable appearance and earnestly tapered, vibraphone-soaked take on bebop represented a pointed rejection of the squalor, seediness and addiction with which so many people associated the jazz scene. The MJQ were not urban, the modern euphemism for African American, but urbane. The next evolutionary stride in jazz came with Ornette Coleman's *The Shape of Jazz to Come* in 1959 — around the same time as Stockhausen's *Kontakte* — a continuous piece of largely improvised playing, whose complex rhythms and fine disregard for the conventions of harmony and chord progression signalled that jazz had reached its own "Schoenbergian" moment. Coleman's "harmolodic" innovation was greeted with bemusement and derision, not just by critics but also by fellow jazz musicians, notably Miles Davis.

The 1950s were a time of consolidation for contemporary classical music in Europe, in France and Italy in particular, with works by composers such as Boulez, Berio, Dallapiccola, Nono and Barraqué exploring and expanding upon the principles of serial music and the practice of electronic and concrète music. Add to that list Gyorgy Ligeti and the former Greek resistance fighter Iannis Xenakis, a trained architect who brought that discipline to his own music making. However, as Hans Stuckenschmidt wrote in *Twentieth Century Music*, "As compositions and styles increasingly deviated from convention and tradition, and as composers pursued ever more some particular principle of style or technique, so the chances of music being comprehended dwindled. The message was still despatched, but it was no longer addressed. At worst, it was a bottle thrown into the sea, its destination unknown." These composers did not go short of commissions, from opera houses and universities, while radio stations in Europe did their conscientious best to support the new music, albeit broadcasting it at a time when most of its listeners were tucked up safely in bed. There were generous sponsors, too, such as the American millionaire Elizabeth Sprague Coolidge. However, the chilly, whistling winds of public indifference could not be ignored — while contemporary European composers did not go hungry, they did go largely unheard.

It is not these Europeans with whom post-war avant-garde music is considered synonymous in today's collective consciousness — they tend to be lumped together as a pack of remorselessly, wilfully opaque atonalists. Rather, it is John Cage. Having studied under Schoenberg, Cage came into his own in 1938 with his works for "prepared piano", in which he introduced foreign bodies such as mallets between the strings of the instrument. A year later, he produced his famous work for turntable, a distant ancestor to hip-hop. His works incorporate *I Ching*- and Dada-derived ideas of chance, indeterminacy (though not improvisation, which was anathema to him). Thinking of Cage, Boulez grumbled in one essay about composers using orientalism as a mask for deficiencies in compositional technique. However, Cage's appeal and charisma transcended music. In a highly capable primer on abstract art, Cage is the only musician, Schoenberg apart, whom the author, Anna Moszynska, considers to be worthy of mention. (She mistakenly dubs his infamous 1954 piece "4 Minutes and 33 Seconds of Silence", which would be to miss the point that the piece is about the impossibility of silence).

Cage was not the sort of musician in whose textures you could luxuriate; he was a conceptualist, whose still, Zen-like works lent themselves perfectly to post-war developments in theatre and art. The way he drained, "unpersoned", "unmusicked" his music was reminiscent of the minimalist tendencies of artists like Yves Klein. He maintained strong links with fellow American artist Robert Rauschenberg, while his performances, in which, for example, radios play simultaneously on different stations in the concert hall, were reminiscent of the Neo-Dada happenings which were a feature of the American landscape around the turn of the '60s.

A reproachful voice from the old, European past, Hans Richter, sounded out against the "Neo-Dadaist" tendencies of American art at this time, which also went under the banners of neo-realism and pop art. Lambasting it for its existential vacuity and "infantilism", he accused the new generation of artists of commodifying the "readymades" of Duchamp, which, he felt, should have been the last, not the first word. However, the American-based Duchamp was now considered a father figure, something he himself resented. "When I discovered 'ready-mades' I thought to discourage aesthetics. In Neo-Dada they have taken my ready-mades and found aesthetic beauty in them."

(NB: All future appraisals of Duchamp's ready-mades should take into account the doubt cast by Barbara Visser's 2023 film, *Alreadymade*, which suggests that the idea for displaying the urinal came from another, lesser known and more ill-fated Dadaist, Baroness Elsa von Freytag-Loringhoven).

The nature of this beauty was a sort of fetishising materialism, however, felt Richter, and the symptom of an overfed but spiritually undernourished civilisation. He cites one modern artist, Daniel Spoerri, who in *Kishka's Breakfast* nails the remains of his girlfriend's hearty breakfast tray to a chair, an assemblage which takes its place in New York's Museum of Modern Art. This he contrasts with Russian artist Ivan Puni's (aka Jean Pougny) 1918 piece *Plate*, part oil painting, part assemblage, which features an empty plate as its central object. "In Russia, in 1918, they were in the middle of a revolution and one potato a day was a lot," writes Richter. "The empty plate was a challenge (to something or someone); the solid breakfast is a satisfaction of something or someone."

These were times when the bourgeoisie, once the object of modern art's scorn, were now among its most enthusiastic benefactors. Nowadays, wrote Brian O'Doherty in the *New York Times* in 1963, the bourgeois reacted to modern art "not with shock, but with pleasure, and by opening its purse." While modern music struggled on, hand to mouth, living off subsidies, modern art was increasingly embraced as a manifestation of the metropolitan super confidence of post-war America in particular, part of the same thrust as Elvis Presley and Coca Cola, spiralling onward and upwards like the Guggenheim museum.

Even the new minimal art was being avidly bought. In 1959, the artist Yves Klein, in a move that was both conceptually immaculate and a canny bit of business, sold zones of his "Immaterial Pictorial Sensibility" — i.e. nothing — in exchange for gold. The minimalist artists of this period aspired to a condition which, as Cage ruefully demonstrated, was beyond music — that of silence. It was meant as a disapproving silence, a withdrawal from the noise of a hyperactive, materialistic society.

However, minimalism has become the great, ironic conceit of the rich — the pretence of a lack of possessions. Walk down any impoverished Third World street, by contrast, and you'll be struck by the maximalism of poverty — the laundry hanging across the pavement, the boiling pots, and the laden mules en route to market, the traders' wares spilling over the pavements, the noisy, sputtering vehicles, the stuff everywhere. These are people without the means suavely to conceal their dependence on the clutter of goods, utensils and transport which, in their case, barely sustains them. Minimalism has become the signifier, in music as well as in art, of capitalism's pretensions to spirituality — some discreetly enabled, airy form of super-being, in which "space" rather than vulgar stuff is the thing.

By 1958, Edgard Varèse's dreams of access to electronic music and sound laboratories had at last been realised. He had already composed *Déserts*, featuring interpolations of musique concrète, based on factory sounds and percussions, like muffled intimations of the outside world as distantly heard from deep in the lonely interior of the soul. Now, he found himself commissioned to compose a piece for the Le Corbusier-designed Philips pavilion at the 1958 Brussels World Fair. Using tape alone, *Poème Électronique*, which was broadcast over 400 speakers, is a sequence of pure electronic sounds and modified spliced recordings of human voices, machines, cathedral bells, pianos and percussion, whose polyphonic assemblage takes you on a slow-moving swoop around and under its great arcs, through an unlit space, in which mysterious, disembodied sounds evoke feelings of awe, fascination and foreboding. Live, the various components would travel along their own "sound routes" from the speakers, adding a dimension of mobility akin to stereo panning. A series of images, including those of mushroom clouds and Charlie Chaplin, were projected onto the walls of the building's interior, though these had no direct relationship to Varèse's work. However, although Corbusier's building (later demolished) received a great many visitors, most of them were confused by both the architecture and Varèse's music. Howard Taubman of the *New York Times* remarked that "the sounds that accompany these images are as bizarre as the building". Although *Poème Électronique* is a surviving monument of musique concrète, its interface with the general public only served to emphasise the difficulty of persuading them to receive in sound-form ideas whose visual equivalent they had relatively little difficulty in embracing.

Still, there were exceptions. In 1958, the American composer and sound engineer Raymond Scott was busy composing jingles and ditties in his own "Manhattan Research Inc.", a sound lab dedicated to designing and manufacturing "electronic music devices and systems". Having already made a reputation for himself, forming the first racially integrated radio band and composing music for Daffy Duck and Bugs Bunny cartoons, Scott would go on to devise, among other things, a prototype for the sequencer. Some of his pieces such as *The Bass-line Generator* were of a serious, experimental bent, but it's his jingles and accompaniments to advertising ditties such as *Lightworks*, *General Motors: Futurama*, *Bendix 1: The Tomorrow People* and *Baltimore Gas & Electric Co.* which are still more remarkable in their juxtaposition of inane, commercial entreaties and innovative electronics which still "sparkle and gleam" to this day, to misquote the lady in the *Lightworks* jingle. Scott later worked with Bob Moog and was even hired by Berry Gordy to work in Motown's electronic music and research department, though none of the recordings he made during that time have ever materialised. Scott was a rare and fleeting example, indeed, of a successful interface between avant-garde music, capitalism and the general public. However, he was only rediscovered two years before his death in 1994, having suffered a stroke and with his royalty stream having long since dried up, when a collection of his long-unavailable work was reissued.

Despite the distaste of Richter and Duchamp, the Neo-Dada ideas in the air in the early '60s found formal expression in the Fluxus movement. The Lithuanian-born artist George Maciunas gave birth to the movement, with an exhibition of works in Germany in 1962. The artists involved came from a range of disciplines including art, music and literature, and hailed from America, Europe and Asia. In contrast to abstract expressionism, which was trumpeted with unseemly patriotism in some quarters as the first Great American art movement, Fluxus prided itself on its crossing of national boundaries. For all that, it does feel American-centred, if one considers New York the receiving centre at this time of the immigration of new ideas. Although it had in common with Dada an idealism, and a desire to bring art and life together and subvert the haute pretensions of the gallery, Fluxus, whose loose coalition were theoretically bound by 12 key ideas, considered itself a constructive rather than nihilistic force.

The childlike and playful tendencies of Fluxus have been well emphasised, and certainly it is hard not to harbour mildly homicidal feelings on reading some of the tracts written in this infantilist vein, such as Dick Higgins's *A Child's History of Fluxus*. Yoko Ono, meanwhile, is capable of exciting similar antipathy for what could be regarded as her loft apartment whimsy. However, one of her schemes rather nicely epitomises the deceptively simple, ingenious, playful and ultimately idealistic spirit of Fluxus — a chess board in which all the pieces are white, so that as the game progresses, the players forget which of the pieces are their own and the adversarial aspect of the game dissolves.

Fluxus represents a high point in the concurrence between art and music. Maciunas had been inspired by the aleatory ideas expounded in the music of John Cage, while one of the key Fluxus tenets was "musicality". This is to say that, much as a piece of music by Beethoven could be orchestrated and reproduced by persons other than the composer, so too could piece of art by, say, George Brecht, be similarly recreated by following the "score" or set of instructions for realising it, set down by Brecht himself. This notion struck at the core of some of art's most sacred tenets — the collectability of the original, the "Do Not Touch" principle. It also meant that, as in music, a given artwork would alter according to who was interpreting it, and when.

Fluxus provided a framework, or perhaps a prism, through which could be understood not just the work of artists such as Joseph Beuys but also composers and musicians such as Tony Conrad, Terry Riley and La Monte Young, the influence of whose unnerving drone music burrowed right into the marrow of The Velvet Underground. Initially, Maciunas showed Breton-like tendencies in his attempting to dictate who or who was not a part of Fluxus, despite its supposed inclusivity. However, he allowed his grip to relent in later years. Perhaps as a consequence of this, it is unclear as to when or whether Fluxus eventually fizzled out. Among its adherents, there is some debate as to whether it has "Unfluxed" or whether it has even yet been born, the world today seeming so far from beginning to take up its tenets. A rather sorrowful open letter testifies to this sense of confusion and also disappointment. Written by one Allen Bukoff, it is entitled "Dear Fluxus" and is addressed to "first and second generation Fluxus among others, Eric Andersen, Henry Flynt, Yoko Ono, La Monte Young, Nam June Paik, Geoff Hendricks and Larry Miller." It begins with Bukoff announcing his departure from the movement, before adding poignantly that most of those artists he lists are unaware that he actually exists, despite his having been an active Fluxus member for many years, operating several websites in the new wilderness of the internet. It's a testimony to a general failure to sustain ideals, a cri de coeur from the enthusiast left behind, and a testament to the inevitable condition of self-absorption rather than social commitment, into which ascended artists also decline. It would be glib, however, to suggest that the ideas of Fluxus have long been assimilated, especially when expressed musically. A few years ago, at the prestigious Meltdown festival on London's South Bank, I saw Tony Conrad, sometime Fluxus associate, perform a piece that essentially consisted of an extended violin solo, oscillating traumatically like a fairground attraction caught in an irreversible lock groove. On and on he oscillated, for 20 or so minutes. When he finally drew to a halt, the auditorium of discerning music lovers was silent, except for one voice crying out more in sorrow than in anger, "You're mad."

Running in parallel to these developments were the advances of jazz into the New of the '60s. John Coltrane, Albert Ayler, Archie Shepp, Pharoah Sanders, Sonny Sharrock, Cecil Taylor and Anthony Braxton were among a new generation at once dismantling the conventions of the jazz idiom at a rapidly exponential rate but also, in many cases (Albert Ayler in particular) recoiled back to the primal rage and lamentation of the blues, as if to suggest that, since the beginnings of African-American music, nothing had fundamentally changed for Black people, with their civil rights still not secure, and the pastoral scenes of the gallant South still disfigured by bigotry. The tuxedoed Modern Jazz Quartet had made their bid for the legitimacy and respectability of the concert hall rather than the nightclub. This transition had become necessary as jazz's avant-garde increasingly failed to serve either its own needs or those of the paying customers in its traditional nightclub setting — it demanded the sort of attention routinely afforded to classical music, the same venues and the same privileges. However, this would be a long time coming. In the early '60s, there was an institutional denial that, despite its dizzying development and increasingly adventurous orchestration, jazz could be considered on a par with classical music. Ornette Coleman and Anthony Braxton often found it impossible to get hired classical players to take their arrangements seriously — they were sniggered at with racist condescension as they presented their scores to symphony musicians complacently steeped in the white, European tradition. For "difficult" white avant-garde composers, it was, well, difficult, to get an airing for their work; for Black composers, it was impossible. Said Chris White, a bass player who worked gigs with Cecil Taylor remarked, "Cecil was forced to work in places where he shouldn't have had to work. And it wasn't because nobody recognised his genius, it's because Black genius isn't recognised — period, in this country."

Players like Coltrane and Albert Ayler were trying to blow down different doors. The impulse, however, was the same — the emancipation of Black people as anticipated, dreamt of, signified, in the emancipation of jazz from its traditional strictures. Coltrane's freewheeling, torrential style, emanating from a body long cleansed of the booze and heroin that had threatened to lay waste to it, reached its apotheosis on the album *Ascension*, in which he truly takes the music to the mountain top. Distributing equal amounts of solo time to a brace of junior saxophonists, Coltrane demonstrated the democratic principles of a new music, moving ever closer to an ideal of pure freedom. Among his acolytes was Archie Shepp, who was fond of saying, "We are not angry men. We are enraged." This summarised the political charge and molten fury which informed the new generation of players. Albert Ayler, who played with a particularly hard reed, was less fluid and ethereal than Coltrane — the noises that emerge from his horn seem to be hewn with a physical difficulty only he is equal to — earthy, honking, chunking blasts, the spirit made flesh and phlegm. There was little need for polemic — themes of struggle, emancipation, evolution, refusing to stand still are embedded in the very warp and wail of the music. To find cross references for the sort of groundbreaking in which the jazz revolutionaries were engaged, you could look to literature, stand-up comedy, even sports in the form of Muhammad Ali and the athlete Tommie Smith. However, there was no similar Black presence in the world of the visual arts, with the solitary exception of the young African-American artist Robert Thompson, who died aged 29 of an overdose in 1966.

The "new jazz" of the '60s was regarded by many with bewilderment; even fellow musicians regarded Ornette Coleman as "crazy", as if mental instability, rather than his desire to dismantle and reinfuse the jazz idiom, explained his decision to play, while other critics lambasted the music for being esoteric, far removed from the concerns of the people whose cause it supposedly sought to espouse, who simply did not listen to it. While it's impossible to disregard some truth in this observation, it denies the fact that Black music's thrust, from Armstrong to Coleman, Hendrix to George Clinton, from hip-hop to dubstep, has always been futuristic, and as such, a reflection of Black experience. On the one hand, Black music is constantly obliged to stay one step ahead of its white imitators (and in so doing, provides a perpetual supply for said imitators). However, it's also because the Black dream is largely one of tomorrow, not yesterday or even today, which aren't generally times on which Black people would particularly want to dwell. Of course, there is reference to the wellsprings of the past but not (at least, until very recently) the nostalgic conservatism that dominates so much white listening and music making. What reason have African Americans to hark back fondly to the good old '60s, the way so many whites do?

One artist who typifies this impulse more abundantly than any other is Sun Ra. Born Herman Blount in Alabama in 1913, Ra could never have entertained any illusions as to what esteem society held him in. Initially a member of Fletcher Henderson's big band, he also became interested in Black Nationalism. However, as he formed his own, unfashionably and oftentimes unfeasibly large ensemble, the Arkestra, he began to construct his own personal creed and mythology based on the ancient past of Egyptology and the remote future of space travel. He carefully erased all traces of his early, Earthly past. Reborn in early middle age, in the 1950s, he now claimed to have come from Saturn.

To be a member of the Arkestra was effectively to take a vow of abstinence and poverty. Players like saxophonist John Gilmore were good enough to have forged titanic solo careers of their own but chose not to out of lifelong devotion to Ra. Stylistically, the band veered between relatively conventional, at times almost quaint bebop-informed big band jazz, theatrical, ritualistic bouts of percussion-driven chanting and zig-zag forays into the outer reaches of new jazz noise, with Ra meandering off on clavichord and electric keyboards.

With their garish, spangly headjoy and robes of many colours, Ra and the Arkestra were, with a handful of honourable exceptions, greeted with bewilderment and amusement by jazz onlookers and enthusiasts at large, if they were greeted at all — Norman Mailer once accidentally stumbled into one of Ra's gigs when in Chicago in the 1950s, and while he credited the Arkestra's piercing "space music" for clearing up his head cold, he later described their music as "strangely horrible". Ra is one of a number of key figures simply overlooked in Ken Burns's 2000 PBS series *Jazz* — impossible to incorporate into that series' earnest, all-American narrative. Many of his fellow African-American musicians regarded him as an embarrassment, playing up to some exaggerated idea of "Blackness" for the delectation of white cognoscenti. Betty Carter snorted that his interplanetary fixations were "bullshit" and challenged him to come up to Harlem and try it on with that stuff. That he chose to use synthesisers was considered an affront to fundamental acoustic jazz principles, too. The path Ra travelled was lonely indeed — it took a singular constitution for him to endure the brickbats, the perpetual economic parlousness and humanity's obdurate resistance to the astral evangelising of *Space Is the Place*.

It's easy to write off Sun Ra as a creature of pure eccentricity. Listen to a track like *The Cosmic Explorer*, a prolonged Ra synthesiser solo that on the face of it sounds like an army of vacuum cleaners hurtling with epileptic frenzy through orbit, and it is easy to imagine that here is a man exhibiting all the signs of mental breakdown, that this is no more than the electronically transcribed hollering of the old bum on the street corner, the epitome of noise-as-madness. But the path Ra travelled wasn't just lonely but also logical. His personal creed and philosophy are best considered as a mythos, a necessary fiction. Everything else about him was altogether serious and quite real. The "Space" to which Ra alluded was a mental solace, for African Americans in particular but for all earthlings living in the shadow of doom in a perilous nuclear age.

Music is far more effective at "visualising", at creating better places, than art. To take just one example from Sun Ra's vast oeuvre — "I'll Wait for You" on the album *Strange Celestial Road*. After a halting opening and a wavering, slightly dishevelled vocal section, in which the Arkestra singers trill wistfully of a world of "abstract dreams", "many lights years in space", where the lucky Arkestra dwell in blissful anticipation of the arrival of the rest of humanity, Ra's keyboards soar and swoop, swallow-like and luminous, above the Arkestra's instrumental scrabble of vibes, wah-wah and undulating percussion below, before taking off in its own right, accompanied by faithful sax lieutenants John Gilmore and Pat Patrick. Ra's keyboards, charting the same courses in spatial infinity as Stockhausen's *Kontakte*, wheel and sparkle, slalom through meteor storms, achieve moments of thermonuclear intensity, navigate their way through wormholes and arc through the colourful gaseous swirls of Hubble telescopic imagery, traverse light years in the mind, and go indeed to places no other music has ventured, staking out, for those curious enough to take the journey, a headzone in which there might be more to life, to human existence, then what has hitherto been decreed by tradition.

If rendered in the form of a painting, "I'll Wait for You" would look corny, the trite, topographic stuff of Yes album sleeves or old, budget sci-fi paperbacks. But this is not a reflection on Ra's aesthetic triteness but on the inherent, comparative capabilities of music and the visual arts to fulfil a particular and vital function — namely to transport, to get us out of this place, not merely as a means of escape but in the hope of some evolution — even if that means, in the imagination at least, leaving planet Earth.

CHAPTER 4

POP ART — FROM MCCARTNEY TO BAILEY

White heat, white noise. The early '60s were dominated by The Beatles, in whom were invested a whole set of soon-to-be-unleashed energies and expectations. They arrived at a time when rock and roll had faltered somewhat, with Elvis's admission into the army taken by many as a signal that the music was a discarded aspect of his, and popular culture's, rambunctious past. Pop was now up for grabs — the label rep at Decca who informed The Beatles that "guitar music was on the way out" was only as out of step as everyone else. It was seriously mooted, for example, in some quarters in the early '60s that the "next big thing" would be a trad jazz revival, as rock and roll, like skiffle, was quietly forgotten about.

The arrival of The Beatles sealed rock and pop's permanency and indefinite hegemony. Their rapid rise to fame, however, wasn't universally celebrated. Beatles monomania came at the expense of diversity within the music scene, with many black artists feeling resentful at being elbowed aside in the scheme of things, and, what's more, with a bowdlerised version of their own music.

However, The Beatles represented a force that could not possibly be denied. And, while it is in the post-1967 phase of their career that they immersed themselves in pop experimentalism and the possibilities of the recording studio, it's in the years 1963–1966 that they offered the most ear-splitting, music-as-noise experience, their cleverly elastic, softly abrasive pop songs played out in live venues against a hysterical wailing wall of adolescent adulation. This was "noise" of a sort unmatched in the more deliberate realms of the avant-garde — uncontrolled, spontaneous and shrill, with a longing that knew not whereof it came. I experienced it once — at a Smash Hits party in London's Docklands in 1995, as a selection of artists ranging from Take That to Radiohead made up an improbable cavalcade. The noise was striking not just in the piercing impact it had on the eardrum but because it was so arbitrary, so unstinting — as if this were a sheer white waterfall that had been raging on for decades, for so long as girl teen adolescence had been wet and unbound. It made indie rock group My Bloody Valentine's experiments in sheer feedback seem a little tame by comparison.

The success of The Beatles was also an indicator of a wider self-confidence in Britain, as it emerged from the post-war austerity years and a long, long winter of Conservative party rule. With Harold Wilson promising a new Britain forged in the "white heat" of technology, the general sense of upswing was felt in all areas of life, from pop to politics, even in town planning, as "new towns" took in the urban overspill and the economy took an upturn. The opening of the first branch of Habitat in London, in 1964, was a harbinger of a newer, smarter, home improvement, more with-it Britain. There was a confluence between the worlds of high art, fashion and design, with architects associated with the brutalist movement now designing the House of the Future at the Ideal home exhibition. Creativity and cutting-edge thinking was the hallmark of this stylish and sanguine era, and much of this was fed by graduates from Britain's art schools, of which there were more, per head, than any other country in the world, attracting young students, often working class, who did not shine academically but had a creative itch they wanted to scratch.

Pop art arose from this context, inspired by the likes of Roy Lichtenstein in America and also as a reflection of the rising tide of consumerism which was at last buoying up the UK. Artists such as Bryan Robertson, Richard Hamilton and David Hockney all represented and refracted the new, affluent over-the-counter culture, in which the "self" was now something you shopped for, in which media, advertising and mass production and the general influence of American culture were making over the very soul of modern Britons. By aping the transience, fashion consciousness and mass produced, youthful, sexy aspects of contemporary life, pop art aimed, in its cutely mobile way, to dispel the un-dynamic, oak-panelled stuffiness of traditional art. Echoes of Dadaism and futurism resound in all of this, and there was, in the best pop art works, a desire to interrogate and deconstruct modern modes of living. Michael Bracewell has described the pop art movement as the vital, missing link between surrealism and postmodernism. Moreover, it was a movement that remained vigilant about the tragic underside of the '60s. Duane Hanson's fibreglass sculpture of a white cop clubbing a Black rioter reflected another consumer reality of the decade — cathode images of American riots beamed through television sets.

Still, for all that, one suspects pop art had its cake of kudos and ate it too. Its wider appeal was to those whose aesthetic preferences were governed by a sweet tooth. When Hockney went to LA and painted ironically banal interior scenes of life there, he may have captured the underlying aridity of the soul in the desert city but he was paid for it in, and accepted, un-ironic truckloads of non-counterfeit dollars. Moreover, pop art chimed in with a newfound sense that the future would be about looking good and a general interest in home improvements. So, Bridget Riley and Mary Quant were part of the same, radical thrust. Fashion, design and what you hung on your walls were all part of the same swing. Mobiles, trompes l'oeils, dress patterns and graphics all merged seamlessly into one another.

The awkward relationship between exhibited art and interior design has persisted to this day. Some time ago, I accompanied a friend of mine around a gallery/shop in London. She was looking to fill some wall space adjacent to her living room doorway. The owner of the place discreetly kept pace with us as we perused, just a yard short of hovering. At one point, my friend expressed admiration for one work, priced at £1500 — a pleasant, abstract piece, vaguely gaseous and billowing, but demurred, as it was in blue, and in order to match the colours of her living room, she was looking for something in, well, a greener vein. At which point, the owner cleared his throat and ventured a suggestion. "Listen," he said furtively, "I know the artist who did this. If you want this done in green, he'll do it in green for you…" Rather than be a party to a young artist's dereliction of their integrity just for £1500 — would Picasso have swiftly converted his blue period into his green one just for a few francs? — we left the gallery.

Arguably, the greater influence exerted by the visual arts, via the art schools, was on British rock music. John Lennon, Ray Davies, Pete Townshend, Syd Barrett and Brian Eno were all products of the English art school system and brought to rock music a colour, shape and sensibility it could not have attained merely by spurs-earning and chops-learning on the conventional gig circuit. Art school musicians were less prone to muso-ism, more to ideas — they would be no more inclined to steep themselves in discussions about this or that guitar than engage in long conversations about paintbrushes. Sometimes the influences of the visual arts surface overtly — in the title of Brian Ferry's solo album *The Bride Stripped Bare*; in Brian Eno's *Oblique Strategies*, devised with Peter Schmidt. The Who's studied delinquency, smashing up their guitars, felt as ritualised and formal as a pop Happening, while their 1968 album, *The Who Sell Out*, with its parodies of adverts for baked beans ads and mock-radio jingles was steeped in pop art mischief. However, the songs on that album emotionally resonate and activate visualisations (*I Can See for Miles*) in a way that spills far above and beyond the conceptual.

The relationship between rock and art can at times be a deferential one — well-fed rock stars who feel the need to elevate their sense of self-esteem rarely do so by producing some expansive, commercially suicidal avant-garde soundscape (though Lou Reed and his *Metal Machine Music* is an exception here). Rather, they try their luck at the easel. Paul McCartney, Bob Dylan, David Bowie, The Rolling Stones' Ronnie Wood, The Stone Roses' John Squire, Bob Dylan and Don Van Vliet, aka Captain Beefheart, are among those who have either exhibited paintings or created their own cover artwork, with varying degrees of success and straight-faced responses. The moment art began to feed rock is the moment the music developed a self-consciousness, a maturity, a sense of its own value and versatility. The relationship has been intermittent and not confined to the UK. The Velvet Underground-Andy Warhol link is an obvious example, while the late '70s and early '80s would see New York artists, musicians, venue and gallery owners briefly rubbing shoulders and sparking off one another during a temporary, never-to-be-repeated dip in Downtown NY loft apartment prices. Jean-Michel Basquiat and Keith Haring, David Byrne and Laurie Anderson were among those who shared a space to mutually fertilising effect.

However, it was in the '60s that the art/rock movement saw rock and roll and pop music lose their innocence, move from showbiz and singles to albums and festivals and develop a long-playing sense of themselves as art forms in their own right. Exposure to art taught them they had the right to think that way. In The Beatles, John Lennon was the art school guy, the one who married Yoko Ono, who made solo albums and contributed individual tracks (particularly the rather amateurish "Revolution 9" on the so-called *White Album*) which convinced many that he was the one who led The Beatles into the second half of the '60s, their longhair, experimental phase. In fact, it is generally accepted nowadays that, despite dazzling contributions, he was something of a passive-aggressive passenger in the late Beatles years and that it was Paul McCartney who was the main, galvanising force in the group. Moreover, it was

McCartney, not Lennon, who exhibited a great deal more interest in the avant-garde musical happenings of the mid to late '60s, under the influence of his future biographer, Barry Miles. According to Miles, in 1966, he witnessed a performance of Luciano Berio's *Thema (Omaggio a Joyce)*. That same year, the composer of *Yesterday* and *When I'm Sixty-Four* was being introduced to, and eating up like hash brownies, the works of Albert Ayler, Stockhausen, Morton Subotnik, John Cage and William Burroughs. And, that same year, he attended a happening in the basement of the Royal College of Art by the free-form group AMM, even contributing to the performance by rolling a coin along the top of a radiator.

AMM arose from the British jazz scene. Saxophonist Lou Gare and drummer Eddie Prévost were members of the Mike Westbrook Band but were intrigued by the developments of free jazz in America. For once — and despite the sneers of EJ Hobsbawm that AMM were "boys" to Sonny Rollins's "man" — what these British musicians produced in response wasn't an anaemic version of the "real thing". Rather, it was beyond jazz, unmoored from its traditions and let loose on open water, a radical extension into the hitherto unexplored realm of total improvisation. This was, in its beginnings, a mostly British phenomenon. The serialist composer Cornelius Cardew became a semi-permanent member of the group, while the American composer Christian Wolff also spent a sabbatical with AMM.

AMMMusic, as the title of their first, 1967, album went, was the result of a collective, highly cerebral reflection on what it meant to make music, which tended to eschew the tenets of modernist rationalism in favour of ... something else. This was in part informed by oriental influences such as TM, Buddhism and gagaku music but, as Eddie Prévost put it, "there was always a sense in which the group itself was the only real vehicle for self-awareness." Despite the thought that went into the idea of what it meant to take part in AMM, the music was spontaneous, unscripted, and the idea of what AMM meant was resistant to analysis. No one could know what the letters "AMM" stood for — no one could know what AMM stood for.

Keith Rowe's cover art was distinctly pop-arty, simple cartoons with lots of primary yellow. The cover to *AMMMusic* depicts a trundling juggernaut marked "AMM", while the cover to 1968's *The Crypt* shows a transistor radio and a blank, yellow speech balloon. From here, the music departed and at times (on *The Crypt* in particular) practically levitated. They were making music, according to Prévost, "as if music were being made for the first time" — and knowing it. Gare's saxophone and violins would hang and whine high above proceedings for minutes at a time; Prévost's percussion would rustle discreetly, then surge, driving the rest of the players along on its waves, as if the very floor were billowing beneath them; Keith Rowe — who developed a "tabletop guitar" technique, rendering his instrument horizontal — provided a sort of canvas upon which his fellow musicians could splash their contributions; Cornelius Cardew would occasionally interject with thoughtful, spartan piano phrases. Completely open-ended, with no melodies, no themes, no regular pulse, simply exploratory playing. It was punctuated by silences, not of the Cageian variety, but lengthy, broody, pregnant pauses, as the group gathered their thoughts and feelings for the next stormy onslaught. These being the '60s, the music was regarded as trancey or trippy, and their performances very often had a hippy informality about them, grist for those who would mark AMM as dated, of their time — at one Berlin concert, held in a church, a young couple thrashed around, making passionate love in the pews during proceedings. But AMM was no mere love-in, be-in, or heavy-eyelidded drugfest but the product of a sober, collective consciousness. No one was having fun, exactly, although AMM was a deeply fulfilling experience for all concerned; this was cultural work. And necessary, too, precisely because of, rather than despite, the sentiment expressed in the title of one of their pieces: *What Is There in Uselessness to Cause You Distress?*

AMMMusic came accompanied by a series of epigrams which arose from group meetings. One was, "An AMM performance has no beginning or ending. Sounds outside the performance are distinguished from it only by individual sensibility." Transistor radios were a key component, therefore, of AMM's music, as if to stress its non-hermetic nature, the way it bled into the world and vice-versa. You could describe AMM's approach as ultra-democratic. Jazz had always been musically conversational, with soloist following soloist, but AMM took this principle to absolute and idealistic extremes. This was what free improvisation meant — not self-indulgence but a free and unfettered exchange of ideas, relevant to the moment, unhindered by customs, traditions or conventions, involving listening and respect for one's fellow players but also disregarding formality. This was music that gave whatever the moment demanded, be it silence or a noisy, choral expression of comment or assent; it was seemingly static but forever shapeshifting. This was music responsive to its own needs rather than any commercial imperatives. There were no stars, no foregrounding of the solo. The individual was subsumed by the collective.

It would be lazy to describe AMM as "free thinking" exactly, as they certainly were not saying, as did the punks 20 years later, that "anybody can do it". Hardly anybody could, insisted AMM.

There was a high turnover of membership, and high standards required, moral as well as musical — cellist Lawrence Sheaff, an early group member, was eased out of the group not least because other members disapproved of his behaviour towards women. And when a group of idiots invaded an AMM concert in Berlin with some ill-advised, inept "free playing" of their own, they were missing the point that to play this music required a rare and exquisite degree of discipline and sensitivity — it would take many months for new members to bed down in AMM.

The idealism of AMM was initially apolitical, but, eventually, the sense that free improvisation provided a metaphor for a model way of living your life may have helped tip members Cornelius Cardew and Keith Rowe over into communism and Maoism respectively. This caused friction within the group, for one senses in AMM, for all their free expression, that there was an underlying English awkwardness about they way they related to each other, which led them to behave in odd ways. The sense of a fatal build-up of emotional reserve was evident, sadly, as late as 2004 when Eddie Prévost openly criticised long-time compadre Keith Rowe for his taking up "electroacoustic" music, in his book *Minute Particulars*. The first Rowe knew of the drummer's thoughts, which may well have masked a deeper ill-feeling, was when he read the book. A rift developed between them which is unlikely to be bridged.

As for Cornelius Cardew, his impassioned idealism went hand in hand with a personal disconnectedness from people. He eventually renounced, in lofty, Soviet-inspired terms, his serialist past; wrote a tract entitled *Stockhausen Serves Imperialism*; formed his own Scratch Orchestra, featuring untutored musicians; and then, towards the end of his life, tried to create an anti-esoteric "People's" music, exhortations to the common man which could be easily bashed out on the piano of any working men's club. Musician Clive Bell recalls seeing Cardew perform in this vein at an Arts Centre. "He said, 'three nights ago I was in East Berlin and I had the honour of writing a song for the Pickle Merchants Union. And this is it'," winces Bell.

"And then he'd thump it out. And it was a hilarious, uncomfortable, post-modern experience. I think he would have come out of it had he not died. He was a faddist, and that was his fad of the moment.

"I think it was a tragedy that he died because I always think had he survived, he would be the one person we'd be seeing on TV talking about modern music. If anyone could have broken through that glass ceiling it could have been him. He was very articulate and very charismatic, and once he'd got past his Maoist phase [...] there's no one like that, now. Gavin Bryars, no. Nyman, no. He could have been the grand old man of the music avant-garde that is currently missing."

One marvels at, even admires Cardew's dedication to his own ideals, even as one chuckles. And, of course, he had precedents. Kurt Weill and Hans Eisler had both abandoned their serious classical training and developed a popular political cabaret style for which they are justly renowned. Cardew, however, was so hopelessly out of touch with prevailing pop mores as to make his own efforts appear comical by comparison.

In 1967, AMM had the same production team as Pink Floyd, including Peter Jenner, who arranged what he later called a "spectacularly shit deal" in order for their debut album to be released through Elektra. Floyd's Syd Barrett sat in on a recording session and doubtless took notes, especially on Keith Rowe's sidelong approach to his guitar and the abstract noises he hewed from it. Paul McCartney, now Syd Barrett. At one point, there was fevered, perhaps retrospective speculation that Keith Rowe had been in line to take Barrett's place in Pink Floyd rather than David Gilmour, but Rowe has recently dismissed this as utter nonsense. There was no more prospect of Rowe joining Floyd than there was of Derek Bailey joining Derek & The Dominoes. Acid-wreck Barrett retired to Cambridge and took up painting. The Beatles and Pink Floyd would sail off in their own directions like ocean liners.

AMM were tugboats by commercial comparison, but they have endured and, one mildly sanitised period at ECM apart, remained rigorously true to their principles — as serious as their lives — throughout their long lives. Parallel to, and independent of, AMM in the 1960s was the Spontaneous Music Ensemble, who were thinking along very similar lines. The SME's number included saxophonist Evan Parker, Trevor Watts, Paul Rutherford and Derek Bailey. Although improv is generally considered a group affair, guitarist Derek Bailey made a decision to work solo for the most part, the better to develop his own style, a "universe unto itself" as his friend Anthony Braxton put it. Bailey's is a remarkable story, and he himself a remarkable character, extraordinarily free of the lofty airs in which "difficult" music is supposed to be steeped. Indeed, he rubbished any of the self-elevation to which all musicians, avant-garde or mainstream, are prone. He unifies experimental practice and the down-to-earthness which is supposed to be its opposite — indeed, Bailey was down to earth to an uncomfortably soiled degree for most. He disassociated himself and his music from the categories of experimental and avant-garde altogether. Far from being an innovator anxious to stay ahead of the field, he considered himself simply to be engaging in the oldest known method of music making.

Bailey's speaking voice was uncannily reminiscent of the veteran British comedian Eric Sykes, and Bailey himself, as a jobbing musician, found himself working adjacent to some of Britain's most high-profile showbiz personalities. He was in the house band of Opportunity Knocks, and also worked with Morecambe and Wise on the road — indeed, on one occasion, Bailey, was ticked off by Morecambe during a show for discreetly practising his singular, improvised fretboard runs during a quiet moment in the middle of a sketch. His everyday work ranged from recording sessions with Tiny Tim to playing for a group of pensioners at Northampton library. In a world in which the rhetoric surrounding art and commerce is often evasive, vague, mealy-mouthed or reeking of cant, he was always open and matter-of-fact about the separation of the need to make a living and the need to involve yourself truly with your music, undistracted by commercial concerns. His was an anti-aura.

Bailey formed a combo in the 1960s called the Joseph Holbrooke Trio, including the composer Gavin Bryars and Tony Oxley, whose moniker has the patina of Brit-jazz respectability about it. But Bailey wasn't interested in extending the jazz tradition — using the likes of Coltrane and Eric Dolphy as a jumping-off place, he wanted to depart from it altogether, into the realms to which he'd been introduced via the works of people like John Cage and Marcel Duchamp, or Anton Webern, whose music he would play at full blast to freak out his Rolling Stones-loving landlady when living in Fulham. The Joseph Holbrooke Trio had about them, said Gavin Bryars, the air of "three northern lads kicking out". As a music, it's more considered than anarchic in the way that it meticulously dismantled expectations — retune your eardrums, adjust to the initial strangeness, and it's possible to make out the way in which Bailey's guitar deliberately falls between the cracks, plumbs new and correct depths of sonority and expression. Each note, each chord was deliberately chosen and arrived at, with decisive flourishes, rather than randomly stumbled upon. Ben Watson, Bailey's biographer, offered the following description of a Bailey collaboration which serves well for his music as a whole: "a continuously evolving junk sculpture which redeems all kinds of ugliness — rust, jagged tears, waste fragments, garish scraps, acid flecks and burns — by a liveliness of placement and contrast." As with AMM, Bailey understood that "free" music didn't mean the admission of any old untutored crap but was the product of a highly evolved condition and attitude towards playing, the expression of a language in which it was necessary to be initiated and trained.

Although Bailey's music features on numerous albums, he himself was uninterested in the end product. "Recording's fine if it wasn't for fucking records," he said, and recommended that buyers of his records listen to them once and then throw them away. Performing, for Bailey, was all about the process. He used the analogy of a jigsaw. "Emptied out of the box, there's a heap of pieces, all shapes, sizes and colours, in themselves attractive and could add up to anything — intriguing. Figuring out how to put them together can be interesting, but what you finish up with as often as not is a picture of unsurpassed banality. Music's like that."

Although AMM were swiftly followed by the Italian ensemble Musica Elettronica Viva (MEV) and Europeans such as Han Bennink, free improvisation has always been a peculiarly British-centred phenomenon. Certainly, the whole scene has mushroomed, with huge numbers of practitioners all over the globe. In America, Sonic Youth have done their best to use their rock star leverage to help disseminate improv. Yet an indomitable Britishness pervades the scene, in the central activities of the London Musician's Collective, in the litany of names of its luminaries — Rutherford, Oxley, Watts, Bailey, Parker — which has the unfortunate side-effect of de-exoticising the music.

With the exception, perhaps, of those pirate radio DJs sending shouts and abstract, frenetic beats out illegitimately across the airwaves, improv is perhaps the least privileged of contemporary cultures. Its inherently evanescent and anti-commercial nature has a great deal to do with this, while the obdurate characters it attracts are hardly likely to be models of consumer friendliness. The music, however, persists, in pubs, on fiftieth birthday parties, on the diminishing scraps fed from the table of the Arts Council, all but ignored. Indeed, it has not just persisted but imperceptibly evolved, subsisting, as ever on the weathered and battered mix of boundless curiosity, hopeless love and good faith of its participants. It can appear sad that, for a music that espouses such communitarian principles, it is riven by internecine squabbling, with what might appear to the outsider to be marginal ideological differences swiftly descending into bitter personal recriminations (as well as the Rowe-Prévost schism, Derek Bailey fell out with Evan Parker). Much of this truculence could be the reaction to the sheer lack of attention afforded to this music — one of the most basic human needs is to be noitced, and it must be hard, indeed, to know that one is so right, to receive consistent critical assurance that one is so right and yet to be so consistently marginalised. And yet, far from being destroyed by internal conflict, free improv continues on its bloody-minded course to nowhere in particular, forever making something out of absolutely nothing.

CHAPTER 5

EUROPE ENDLESS, POST-PUNK TO THE '90S — THUS FAR, NO FURTHER

Following the Second World War, America's cultural sway was unrivalled, whether in pop or as patron of the arts, or as disseminator of new art forms such as jazz and rock and roll, channelled to Europe like a sort of cultural Marshall Plan. This was certainly the case in West Germany. There, it took until the late 1960s for a generation to grow up with no personal involvement with the Nazis, who felt disdainful of their parents, who refused to address the issue of their own guilt or implication, but merely grazed on American dollars, or perhaps did the twist to American Forces Network radio, hoping that a cloud of amnesia would bear them along into the future.

Many young Germans were happy to go along with this plan. However, a more sceptical fringe decided it was time for their country to undergo a reawakening. In the case of the Baader Meinhof Group, this meant a violent assault on the rotten props upon which the West German state was borne upright, be they Nazi-tainted civic leaders or the capitalistic, overweening influence of the Americans. For others, this would be expressed through music, as a means of laying new cultural foundations. This was what prompted the rise of the so-called "krautrock" movement, in which various key groups, working independently of each other, strove to create a newly reconfigured rock music which didn't merely ape the latest American imports. Although Germany had been physically rebuilt, spiritually it was in ruins. Thanks to the war, a generation had effectively gone missing, been disabled, struck mute. "We had no Fathers," said Ralf Hütter of Kraftwerk, summing up this feeling of being culturally orphaned. For Hütter, one of the few people they could point to for surrogate parentage was Stockhausen. This was the case also for Can, whose members included Holger Czukay, a former pupil of the composer. Stockhausen's initial striving for a materially wholly new music, electronic in origin, was borne out of idealism, a need to begin again, that was a direct response to the horror of the recent war. Now, the next generation would import this idea of a new music, original and German in origin, into more popular realms.

Two key groups, Can and Faust, were both inaugurated in the same way — cloistered away from society, in commune-type dwellings, there to dedicate themselves to constructing from scratch an entirely new music. Despite looking to escape American hegemony, Can were in part inspired by The Velvet Underground, whom Irmin Schmidt saw in New York, where, touched by the minimalist spirit, they had found a way of reducing rock to its first principles, its Black essence. Can arose from lengthy, riffing jam sessions undertaken at the Schloss Nörvenich — they were the inverse of conventional prog rock, whose lengthy, instrumental passages noodle outward, on spurious cosmic odysseys. Can tunnelled inward, into "Inner Space", as the name of their studio had it. Their early work is primal, repetitive, with locked rhythms — yet open-ended, allowing for Michael Karoli's guitars to flow freely across verse-less and chorus-less terrain, and for Irmin Schmidt's keyboards to provide not just texture but also unexpected events and changes in direction. Over all this hung the vocalist Malcolm Mooney, a Black fugitive from the Vietnam War who sang as if entranced, up to his neck in the music lapping around him. It's unfortunate that his mental health wasn't the most robust — his last gig saw him locked in a mind-groove of his own, chanting over and over the words "Upstairs, downstairs", as if he had been caught in the trap of one of Jaki Liebezeit's perpetually repetitive drum riffs. He left and was replaced by Damo Suzuki, a young Japanese busker whose more featherweight vocals airlifted Can into a new lightness of being, as evinced on their 1973 album *Future Days*. Can offered rock a potential redesign, showed how by freeing up the traditional interrelationships between drum and bass, lead instruments and vocals, rock could be liberated from its hackneyed old trad tropes and ascend into a weightless, but not formless state.

Faust were originally the concept of journalist Uwe Nettelbeck, who soldered together the stray members of two late '60s German groups into a new collective, which, he persuaded the German branch of the Polydor label, could be nurtured into the "new Beatles" — which is to say, not moptops with umlauts but a group that would, in the novelty of its approach, have the same impact The Beatles had had in the 1960s. Unwisely, from a commercial perspective, Polydor greenlit Nettelbeck and the members of Faust (whose name alluded both to the human fist and to Marlowe's doctor) gathered at Wümme, a compound that had once been a school, and set up studio. There was much carousing, bringing home of friends and general social laxness. There was also a good deal of jamming, with free rock pummelled into shape by the Leviathan percussion of Werner Diermaier and strafing, billowing interventions of analogue synthesiser, buffeting amidships delicate compositions like *Meadow Meal*. Faust felt like a latter-day Dada soundtrack in their use of aleatory "exquisite corpse" lyrical techniques, their use of collage, noisy broadside, their iconoclasm (the opening of their first, self-titled album sees samples of The Beatles and The Stones dissolved in an acid bath of analogue synthesiser crackle) as well as a plaintively insistent pastoral strain, denoting a simple, pacifistic belief which refused to be soiled or wither away. Can and Faust were among a number of groups who flowered in Germany, whose hippy culture was particularly forthright and persistent, perhaps as a reaction to events two generations earlier. Largely ignored or condescended to by an Anglo-American industry and media still misguidedly fixated on the more "important" developments of progressive and heavy rock. The over-elaborate, overblown aspirations of Pink Floyd, Genesis, Deep Purple (who can forget their *Concerto for Group and Orchestra*?) to a "classical" status were based more on length, grandeur and virtuosity than any radical investigation into what it meant to make music and what shape it should take.

Kraftwerk were formed a little later than Can and Faust and, initially, were as free playing and longhaired as their German contemporaries. However, by the mid-1970s, they had settled into a four-man unit that played on electronic instruments, dressed in business suits and paid disingenuous tribute to the feats of the modern, technological age. They received widespread exposure through an appearance on BBC TV's *Tomorrow's World* in 1975, but for many this also signified their supposed novelty — they were to be taken no more seriously than Rolf Harris's Stylophone. That they were German in the 1970s was, of course, held to be amusing in itself, as was reflected in contemporary profiles of the band. Kraftwerk responded by feyly playing up their Teutonicism, especially in one notorious interview with Lester Bangs. Kraftwerk bemused and offended in their rejection of rock's sacred tenets — their insistence on suits and ties, their deliberate effeminacy (on the constructivism-inspired sleeve to 1978's *The Man-Machine*, they sported rouge lipstick), which in the rock mind was of a piece with their rejection of the guitar, a wanton act of self-emasculation. The faintest smile played about the lips of Kraftwerk, despite their ostensibly grand demeanour. They knew what they were doing, what hackles they were raising. Although they dressed conservatively, they realised that rock music, for all its posturing of rebellion, was at heart the true conservative, especially in its attachment to the electric guitar, clinging to it as anxiously as a man who habitually clutches his own crotch. The mistrust of keyboards, mere sound creators rather than heroic, Phallic Axes was another sore point for Kraftwerkophobes, and indeed continues to be so to this day in America, where synthesised sounds are considered inauthentic, signifiers of ephemerality and possibly homosexual tendencies. Machines are things you rage against, not enter into alliances with. To Kraftwerk, this was so much Luddite nonsense. As Ralf Hütter told me when I interviewed him in 1991, the people who castigated them for using new technology did not have the same misgivings when it came to their own dental treatment.

Kraftwerk were playing a joke on the meatheaded, open-necked, hoary rock mindset, but they themselves were no joke. Quite contrary to mid-'70s expectation, which imagined that the future would be one of still wider flares and triple fretboard guitars, they were engaged in the electrification of modern pop music, pretty much all of which rides on the rails they laid down — as well as setting up the template for hip-hop, when their influence was belatedly taken up by Afrika Bambaataa in 1982. Indeed, once their work was done in this regard, they fell silent — since the mid-1980s, their output has been minimal.

Can and Faust both fell idle in the late 1970s but were revived in the post-punk generation, when it turned out that the likes of Julian Cope, John Lydon, Mark E Smith and The Buzzcocks' Pete Shelley were all huge krautrock fans, despite the supposed amusicality punk was supposed to stand for. As they were increasingly name-checked, their influence began to pervade in earnest, and both groups even reformed, Can briefly in 1989 and Faust from 1993 onwards. Still, for mainstream listeners steeped in the Anglo-American hegemony, it was unthinkable that the new music should come from the old Europe, crumbling and discredited. Who, after all, won the war?

Krautrock is part of an alternative rock lineage, in which form and process take precedence, in which texture is as important as, indeed often more important than, text. The two lineages aren't mutually exclusive, of course — The Beatles were as alternative as they were mainstream, for example; Hendrix as mainstream as he was alternative. Nevertheless, cast an aerial eye along the white lines of mainstream rock's grey road and it goes something like: Elvis, The Beatles, The Stones, Bob Dylan, Neil Young, David Bowie, The Sex Pistols, Elvis Costello, The Smiths, R.E.M., U2, Oasis, all part of a great, heroic, narrative tradition, even though each has, in some way, revolted violently against orthodoxy. These are honourable men in the main, even though, in this writer, such a list induces stirrings of ennui and a mild nausea at its odours of heritage and tradition, the floor polish of the Hall of Fame. But then there is another tradition, an anti-tradition, whose names include The Mothers of Invention, Captain Beefheart, Jimi Hendrix, Can, Faust, Kraftwerk, Brian Eno, Cabaret Voltaire, Suicide, This Heat, PiL, The Associates, Yello, The Young Gods, My Bloody Valentine, Sonic Youth, Radiohead, by which point the line has long since tangled up and tapered off into a thousand threads. The names in this second list are famous ones, yet as rock ossifies into retroism, and decade by decade musical retrospectives focus increasingly on a decreasing canon of all time greats, then this whole anti-tradition is becoming increasingly marginalised.

What is considered unorthodox about the second list of rock artists is that which is considered perfectly orthodox in the twentieth-century visual arts — that is to say, their impatience with conventional or received modes of expression and their constant search for new permutations, fresh juxtapositions and new means of unleashing content. The Mothers of Invention are generally regarded as the great avant-garde rock revolutionaries of the 1960s, with Frank Zappa matching scatology, iconoclasm and fiendish virtuosity, as well as an effortless eclecticism, which took in every mode of music from doo-wop to serialism. He was an influence and an inspiration. And yet, Zappa is, in many ways, as inappropriate a countercultural spearhead as André Breton.

Zappa wasn't exactly a free spirit. He was an autocrat. He was fiercely anti-drugs. His attitudes to women oscillated between lechery and social conservatism. Even as his players let rip, belch or wig out, you feel they're doing so within a tightly scripted framework. Though he couldn't sing, his voice is everywhere on his records, often in the form of a flat and snide narrative; his lampooning of pop mores, especially on later tracks like *Disco Boy*, reeks of above-it-allness. When he goes on some elaborately arranged, dazzlingly speedy jazz/rock foray of his own, it's as if his prime motive is to demonstrate his superiority. Doo-wop melted his heart, but he slaps it about satirically in his early records. The problem with Zappa is that he didn't appear to have a Dionysian fibre in his being. He was an artisan, a satirist, and technically very gifted — he simply lacked a soul. It's an unfortunate little quirk that Zappa, for many, is the historical poster boy of the rock avant-garde — that famous photo of Zappa on the crapper, the "Z" for zany, the easily cartoon-rendered little moustache and beard.

Zappa wasn't immersive. That's not something you can say of Don Van Vliet, aka Captain Beefheart, the "Zig Zag Wanderer", at whose crossroads Howlin' Wolf, Ornette Coleman and The Mad Hatter meet. His 1969 album, *Trout Mask Replica*, Simpsons creator Matt Groening's favourite album of all time, is a trove of new tangents, wormholes and trapdoors available to rock and roll, all of which come from shock exposure to that which preceded it (the blues) and that which came after it (free jazz). Thirty-seven years after its making, you would think its lessons would have been absorbed, its serrated edges worn away by time and tide. But no. In 2006, John Harris of the *Guardian* wrote a piece in which he recounted setting himself the supposedly daunting task of listening to the double album. He found himself unequal to it. "Its opening moments let you know what you're in for: a discordant racket, all biscuit-tin drums and guitars that alternately clang and squall, eventually joined — apparently by accident — by a growling man complaining that he 'cannot go back to your land of gloom'. Skipping through the remaining 27 tracks does not throw up anything much more uplifting." In fairness, Harris persisted gamely with *Trout Mask Replica* rather than merely dispensed with it, interviewed musicians like Gary Lucas and Andy Partridge in search of insight into what to him seemed to be its arcane impenetrability, explored some of the more accessible Beefheart works. However, you still sense that his inability to get to grips with *Trout Mask Replica* is generally symptomatic of the conservative condition of twenty-first-century Britpop rock, that in which the unpredictable bend of a guitar chord is once again as shocking as the glimpse of a stocking.

Jimi Hendrix's influence has been solar. Having toiled in the backlines of American soul and rhythm and blues outfits for some years, he was re-launched in England by his management team as the new "wild man of rock", an object of almost zoological fascination. His gimmicky, highly sexed onstage style, and the mildly racist manner in which he was sold (exhibited?) to the British public initially overshadowed the sheer molten magnificence of his playing — the blues dipped in red-hot technology to create a *Purple Haze*. Hendrix may not have been the first guitarist to incorporate feedback into his playing, but he was certainly the first to disseminate it widely. Hendrix's guitar work feels like action painting — this wasn't rock music inscribed with a thin nib but applied in extravagant brushstrokes. This wasn't a group; this was an *experience*. Hendrix rarely played acoustic guitar — his medium was electricity. Abetted by every new piece of technology he could lay his hands on, he hurls, sprays and spatters sounds, drenches the listener with colour, with what at times borders on sheer eddying, tornado noise. As well as being the conduit for all the firestorms and electric tension of his era — he himself is the visual realisation of his music (he has always been a particularly attractive subject for artists, amateur and otherwise). The very obvious use of his instrument as a metaphor for sexual potency can't be overlooked, but Hendrix's music is emancipatory rather than merely ejaculatory. Every bank is broken, every door blown off its hinges, every pore unclogged, every precedent reduced to cinders. After Hendrix, the white thread of '60s music sounded skinny and anaemic by comparison. For all the invention of The Beatles in the late '60s, they couldn't compete sonically after 1968's *Electric Ladyland*. George Harrison's gently weeping guitar was no match for this.

The Who and Eric Clapton quaked in their boots and attempted to raise their game as best they could.

Hendrix is very often associated with the era of protest, but, as an ex-paratrooper, he only abandoned his pro-Vietnam War stance late in the '60s. As an individual he was mild-mannered, even deferential. However, his music represents the torrential expression of a long-suppressed, long-sublimated cocktail of inner emotions rage among them. Hendrix's immediate legacy was a trawl of technically proficient, masturbatory white longhairs, who dominated the prog rock years, while his raising of the volume and temperature of rock helped enable heavy metal (a genre that has actually matured but was, in its early, denim and poodle-haired pomp, godawful and troglodyte). Strangely, he didn't inspire a great deal of Black rock — Living Colour are cited as descendants of Hendrix, but it's hard to cite more than a handful of others. The significance of Hendrix was that he brought to rock something that no white player ever could by virtue of being African American and all that that entails, from the social privations to the musical traditions he soaked up. Rock critics of a conservative strain, those who don't wish the genre to stray too far or become too processed, who like their music "tight" and "raw", tend to favour early Hendrix. However, it's in his later works, in which he really spread himself out, that he gives us his full measure — in works like *1983 … (A Merman I Should Turn to Be)*, a fantasy about retreating into an undersea utopia to escape a broken world, a fantasy realised in the oceanic, turquoise shades and brilliantly engineered soundwork of the piece. Or in *Voodoo Chile*, a Promethean monument to African-American potency and rage, cut in 1968 — the year Martin Luther King Jr was assassinated, the year of athlete Tommie Smith's Black power salute at the Mexico Olympics — which was issued as a single in 1970 following Hendrix's death and reached number one in the UK charts. Or his version of *The Star Spangled Banner*, not so much a rendering as a rending, an act of fretboard flag-burning needing no explanation. Hendrix represents one of the few and precious instances of noise music rocking the world on its axis, or at least reflecting the giddy, seismic times.

In 1977, the same year that Jacques Attali wrote his seminal text, *Noise*, UK punk was just blowing itself out, having done its levelling best to demonstrate Plato's dictum that, "When the mode of music changes, the walls of the city shake." That shake might well have been the mere bristle of manufactured moral panic, but the implications of punk, if not its original, rude blast, were profound. Rock's lineage and hierarchy, its modernistic sense of progression based on hermetic and elitist notions of advanced musical proficiency, had been brought crashing down. Moreover, punk was arguably the soundtrack to late capitalism in deep crisis. It was the noise of those deemed surplus to requirement — the people who made it were useless, as citizens and as musicians. From this would spring punk's vitality.

And yet, punk's "back-to-basics" ethos was as reactionary as it was radical, as the New York synth duo Suicide discovered to their cost. In 1978, Suicide, who consisted solely of vocalist Alan Vega and a sun-glassed Martin Rev on synths, supported The Clash on their On Parole tour in the UK. Vega's sultry, Elvis impersonator rockabilly tones were supplemented by the skeletal, ghostly hiss of Rev's drum machine and fuzzy, sawn-off keyboard riffs. This was beyond "basics"; this was rock reduced to its absolute, minimal essence, its pulse. And the British punks, apoplectic with aesthetic offence, were not having it. Night after night, Suicide were showered with bottles, glasses, spittle, even footwear (did the perpetrators come pre-armed with shoes, or face an uncomfortable walk back home?), an unrelenting shower of Americanophobic, technophobic antipathy. Punk is often crudely caricatured as a roar of working class discontent, a political protest, when in fact it was a protest against the dark tedium of British '70s life, not least under the Labour Government, as well as what was perceived as the musical choice it offered between Pink Floyd and The Bay City Rollers, which was no choice at all. It and Thatcherism were arguably two sides of the same coin — indeed, one or two punks, including

The Jam's Paul Weller, declared, albeit more out of flippancy than political conviction, that they would be voting Conservative in the 1979 general election. Joy Division's Ian Curtis did so also, cheekily cadging a ride to the polling station from the local Liberal candidate.

Punk tapered off in various directions: into New Wave, a sanitised, poppier mutation; into Oi!, an imperviously lumpen continuation of punk's three chord shoutiness, for those who regarded punk as a terminus rather than a new beginning. It was post-punk, however, which saw it take its most significant evolutionary turn. Post-punk matched a newfound and urgent political articulacy with musical openness. If punk had been the detonation, post-punk operated in the smouldering crater it left behind. Post-punk was sombre, avant-garde, interrogative. If punk had been the Big Bang, then this was the expansion. Post-punk was at once about intensity, an over-used word but never inappropriate in the case of Joy Division, but also about irony. Pop was now "pop", its innocence now obliterated; rock was now "rock", its '60s-born pretension to superiority discredited. All channels were now open to other genres, other ethnicities, other decades.

As had happened with Suicide, it was the punks who were most enraged by post-punk's extremes, not least because they were perpetrated by ex-punks. Wire, for example, though signed as an art rock band, were perceived as punks following their debut, 1977's *Pink Flag*, and its two minute gobbets of raucous guitar pop, culminating in the blistering *1 2 X U*. But Wire were singularly artful in their music-making. Although highly appealing, acidic and honeyed by turns, there was a strong element of cartographic calculation about them, as evinced in one of their greatest songs, *Map Ref. 41°N 93°W*, from *154*. Their songs were deployed, rather than emoted. By 1979, they sought to detach themselves from their hardcore following, still braying for the old hits from *Pink Flag*. 1979's *Document and Eyewitness* records one of their final gigs. Amid half-formed songs that threaten to break down into industrial, ambient drones, the gig was punctuated by bits of performance art, reminiscent of Dada happenings. According to the sleeve notes, *Piano Tuner (Keep Strumming Those Guitars)* is accompanied by the instruction "Vocalist attacks gas-stove", while the sarcastically stillborn instrumental, *Everything's Going to Be Nice* is supplemented by "Woman enters pulling 2 tethered men and an inflatable jet". The purpose of all this seems to have been to tease and provoke, as if shamelessly to rub the punk audience's loathing of all things "pretentious" and "arty" in their faces.

John Lydon had always wanted to be more than the yob on the end of a leash he was taken for in The Sex Pistols. Public Image Ltd gave vent to his profound, nihilistic scornfulness and revealed a highly developed sensibility — his epiphanies had occurred while listening to reggae and European avant-garde rock like Can and Magma during the '70s. The mighty rhythm section of drummer Martin Atkins and bassist Jah Wobble would function as a trampoline for his and guitarist Keith Levene's vaulting ambitions. These would involve some Gesamtkunstwerk-style attempts at mixed media events which they didn't really have the stamina to follow through, as well as ambitions, key to post-punk as a whole, to dismantle rock music itself (the term "rockism" was coined during this era — rock became a dirty, hoary word). PiL's efforts would culminate in *Metal Box*, in which Lydon's spleen and inner turmoil — at the Troubles, at the death of his mother, at the "layered mass of subtle props" which sustained the blandly illusory, hypocritical state of bourgeois things in the UK — was accompanied by a soundtrack of anti-pop, dub, scalding, aluminium guitars courtesy of Levene. Live, Levene would use the Prophet 5 synthesiser to strafe the likes of *Careering* and *Theme* with invasive, disfiguring streaks of analogue noise, to the bewilderment of some audiences whose definition of noise amounted merely to three chord rambunctiousness — or to the rapt terror of Annie Nightingale on BBC's *The Old Grey Whistle Test*. Lydon's notoriety saw to it that PiL's abrasions made it all the way to *Top of the Pops*.

Noise was at the gates of Rome. America's own punk movement, though less iconoclastic than its UK variant, threw up Pere Ubu.

While most punters opted for the skinny, leather-jacketed, radically ultra-orthodox Ramones, Cleveland's Pere Ubu (their name a throwback to proto-Dadaist Alfred Jarry's scandalous play *Ubu Roi*) were a different proposition, despite sharing US punk's rock rush. Ubu, their corpulent frontman and lyricist David Thomas in particular, projected uncoolness. They rocked like jelly, Thomas's lyrics gibbering with giddying existential self-consciousness, physical awkwardness, constantly grasping in vain for footholds in the "real world" which seemed forever just beyond reach. Always tracking Thomas's vocals were the unique emissions of Allen Ravenstine's analogue synthesiser, whose synaptic bleeps, blips, shrieks and weirdly granular configurations were once compared by a critic to the "sound of Pere Ubu's brain". Synthesisers had been used plenty of times as a supplement to rock music but never in such a tangential, unearthly manner as this.

There were groups, too, who were "post-punk" even though they'd been around since before punk was invented, such as Throbbing Gristle and Cabaret Voltaire, as well as groups who were considered themselves as part of a separate experimental rock trajectory, who nonetheless through accident of place and time fell into the rhetorical corral of post-punk — This Heat were prominent among them. Throbbing Gristle's background was in performance art, as part of COUM Transmissions, an art ensemble that specialised in art designed to bridge the moat that traditionally separates artist and audience, with performances legendarily involving maggots, injected genitalia, dildos and soiled tampons as part of their gruellingly immersive experiences. They then decided that, in order to bring their ideas to a wider audience, they should form a group — a sort of anti-group, in that none of its members could particularly play. Instruments were a means for conveying ideas rather than demonstrating skills. Their most famous song, if song is the word, was *Discipline*, which vocalist Genesis P Orridge demanded with a sort of double-edged irony, over a whiplash drum machine riff and coruscating, corrugated textures of guitar and synthesiser. At the turn of the decade, they found themselves playing at the Lyceum. As group member Cosey Fanni Tutti recalled when I interviewed a reformed (but unrepentant) Throbbing Gristle in 2007, they decided to test the room by using noise as a sort of flamethrower, a purge. "The first half an hour was noise, just to drive away all the liggers and Spandau Ballet clones. See how committed are you; can you get through this for ten minutes?" Throbbing Gristle had been described by an irate Tory MP as "Wreckers of Civilisation" following a 1976 ICA exhibition, and despite accusations of gross morbidity (a song about a burns victim) and dabbling in holocaust imagery and their overall toxic fragrance, they considered themselves highly ethical, dedicated to the idea of "deconditioning", as William Burroughs had it — encouraging listeners to evade the preset circuits of modern society in which they were apt to become unwittingly entrapped, using various tactics, shock and satire among them.

Cabaret Voltaire were less ideological than Throbbing Gristle, in interviews at least, but their early records in particular (which featured future field recordings specialist Chris Watson), conceived at their Western Works studios, were uniquely configured. They used percussion, guitar and vocals, but they eschewed melody, verse and chorus in favour of a driving, surging, repetitive and enjoyably oppressive momentum, through which samples (in advance of the invention of sampling machines), shards of electronic and unsheathed bursts of instrumentation hung high and phosphorescent in the mix. In those times, stricken with anxiety about Cold War, recession, the idea that some ideological or technological blunder could plunge the world into thermonuclear annihilation (as, it later emerged, very nearly happened in 1983), and with 1984 just around the corner, Cabaret Voltaire's music, shot through with Mallinder's snarling vocals, was the very sound-picture of sweat-soaked foreboding. Were it not so bleakly compelling, listening to it would amount to masochism.

This Heat had a sort of pariah status even within the world of independent music on which they peripherally hovered. On one occasion, they were playing a support slot and announced to a crowd clearly impatient for their departure that this would be their "last number" — before embarking on a 25-minute session of gruelling improv. They made a connection with the more avant wing of prog rock, including the Canterbury Scene (drummer Charles Hayward's vocals recall those of Robert Wyatt), but their slogan — "All possible processes. All channels open." — was more post-punk than post-punk itself in its implications. Squat dwellers, they believed, Dada-style, that nothing was inadmissible as a source of music. Their *Health and Efficiency* features an extended conclusion in which, over an obsessive, sawn-off, mantra-like riff, the recorded noises of milk bottles, sundry jetsam and the street sounds emanating from outside their Fridge recording studio all collapse into the mix as valid interjections. This was of a piece with their desire to "do violence to accepted notions of music".

Added to these names, in the late '70s and early '80s, could be those of 23 Skidoo, Nurse with Wound, Einstürzende Neubauten (who took up where Faust had left off in the '70s, taking drills and chainsaws to rock's accepted fixtures and fittings — literally, in the case of the ICA), the Mnemonist Orchestra, Lydia Lunch, Robert Rental, Milk from Cheltenham, among others. It wasn't just that post-punk was a creative, countercultural surge brought on by particularly troubled times; it was that it had a profile. Thanks to the efforts of a raft of enthusiastic writers working for a healthy-selling music press, including *Sounds*, *Melody Maker* and particularly the *NME*, these groups, daringly avant-garde, had access to a wider audience, which they probably would not have enjoyed in our own times of enforced incuriosity. Peter Rehberg, founder of the Vienna-based Mego records, was just one of many who were introduced not just to the new music of the early '80s but also to the music it referenced, by the music press of the day. (In 1983, the *NME* put Sun Ra on the cover. Such a departure for that magazine would be utterly unthinkable nowadays.) Furthermore, the *NME* encouraged the idea that from ABC, The Associates, PiL and The Teardrop Explodes at the apex of the charts to the industrial likes of Throbbing Gristle there was a continuum, as if they were part of them same, broad cultural project, with punk as the catalyst.

This writer, as a young reader, quite earnestly believed that post-punk represented, should the planet survive, the beginnings of a new period of evolution for rock music. Rock's ingrained sexism, its hidebound clichés had been exposed and surgically removed, forever. Now that everyone knew better, such things would no longer recur. The privileged status of guitars and the white rock narrative tradition had been revoked. The verse-middle-bit-chorus rules had been bent double like rods of iron over the knee of post-punk thinking. The channels that had been opened would remain open and be extended and expanded with each succeeding generation. What had once been considered "noise" would now rush through these channels as naturally as water. Post-punk would do to previous music at the end of the century what the avant-garde had done to figurative art at the beginning.

This, however, would prove to be as ill-founded as prog rock's complacent belief that prog would simply get progger and progger, sideburns thicker and thicker, flares wider and wider. The first hint of "unvolution" would occur while, one by one, Lydon would abandon his PiL members and revert to a carrot-haired parody of his former punk status. PiL would gradually be reduced to a session band as Lydon, once so venomously acute, began to degenerate into an old punk diva, grandly dispensing jaundice in his impending middle age from his out-of-touch Los Angeles perch. By 1996, he was involved in a lucrative but otherwise ill-advised Sex Pistols reunion.

Dave Rimmer once wrote a book called *Like Punk Never Happened*; however, until the last few years, it has been Like Post-Punk Never Happened. Even nowadays, in the TV retrospectives which are playing an increasing and frequent role in sealing a simplistic version of music history, post-punk, too nuanced for the small screen in even its most poppist manifestations, is leapfrogged over in timelines that jump from punk to Duran Duran, then on to Acid House, followed by Nirvana then Britpop, followed by an awkward silence. Despite the profound influence it has wrought on groups such as LCD Soundsystem, The Rapture and Franz Ferdinand among others, there is a preference in the simplified, exalted upper echelons where John Lydon nowadays dwells that post-punk, in particular its ramifications, not be discussed.

Still less likely to be discussed was a brief recrudescence of "noise", as music as a thing-in-itself, in the late '80s and early '90s. In the mid-'90s, indie groups cultivated a deliberate smallness, as if too much irony intake had resulted in stunted growth. Groups like The Wedding Present and The Housemartins reflected this tendency. Even The Smiths, despite Johnny Marr's luminous excellence and Morrissey's undoubted charisma, were deeply reactionary, almost radically regressive. Morrissey's wistful celebrations of a monochrome Britain, of Kitchen Sink icons and Sandy Shaw, bespoke a horror at the subsequent, gaudy "colourisation" of pop music. Moreover, his avowed disdain for Black music, from reggae to Diana Ross, plus lyrical flirtations with far-right culture (*Suedehead*, *The National Front Disco*) led to recurring accusations of racism. Certainly, it's fair to say that he personally rejected some of indie music's more open dalliances with funk, soul, reggae, etc. He always preferred a resiliently Caucasian, traditionally wrought, guitar-driven style. He has been enormously popular as a result.

However, there was a massive, burgeoning counterweight to all this. In America, Big Black, Sonic Youth and Butthole Surfers in particular reinvested rock with an unapologetic sense of its own hugeness and, if not destiny, then certainly density. If there was an antecedent for Big Black, it wasn't the obvious — punk, hardcore, thrash, etc. — but *Blank Frank*, Brian Eno's collaboration with Robert Fripp on *Here Come the Warm Jets*. Big Black's Steve Albini simply and methodically unleashed his guitar into the air, un-anchored by the dreary tropes of heavy metal or the fist-clenching "attitude" of US hardcore. It was about the noise, in all its sculptured, trepanning awesomeness. Butthole Surfers offered a sacrilegious, misshapen regurgitation of the heavy rock of Led Zeppelin and Black Sabbath, cubistically distorted in the hindsight of the '80s. Sonic Youth, meanwhile, starting from an ostensible Velvets-esque bubblegum stance, worked up to a haemorrhaging frenzy of noise and improv, bridging the gap between Lollapalooza and Sun Ra and all points beyond. No other major rock group, incidentally, has done as much to try to open up channels between rock and the avant-garde, which has not always effectively reciprocated this curiosity.

In the UK, meanwhile, The Jesus & Mary Chain arrived in the moderate climate of the British indie scene amid a hailstorm of feedback. This in turn inspired AR Kane, a Black duo who drew on feedback, Miles Davis's oceanic tendencies, dub and psychedelia to create a homebrewed, highly effective "dreampop", in which nectarine streams of melody were assailed by acid storms of guitar. And then came My Bloody Valentine, who made an improbable metamorphosis from cutie strawberry indiepoppers into the calm perpetrators of the most extreme extraction of guitar sound ever witnessed in the broad realms of rock, a sound which came at you in wave after white wave, not derived from feedback, or psychedelia — rather, a noise from nowhere. In fact, guitarist-cum-sound technician Kevin Shields achieved his sound through a technically prosaic but highly effective mix of techniques, including overdubs, bass distortion pedals, sampled and reprocessed feedback, channelling a tremolo through a Fairlight V2000. He was no great theatrician, like Hendrix, but much as 1991 was the year long jumper Mike Powell finally exceeded Bob Beamon's 8.90 long jump of Mexico 1968, so Shields finally exceeded, in 1991, with *To Here Knows When*, the Richter Scale levels achieved by Hendrix in 1968 on *Voodoo Chile*. Neither mark has been approached since. *To Here Knows When* achieves the sort of hurricane Neil Young could only sing about. Somewhere, like Captain Oates stumbling away in a blizzard, the faint form of a song can be made out. Vocalist Bilinda Butcher sings enervatedly, as if dazed and bled by the tremolo furies raging around her. This was a supernova, a wipe-out — and, given that it featured on the *Tremolo EP* which made it into the Top 30, it was, technically, a hit, part of the Pop Parade. Nothing like it has made such a close approach since. Nor has Shields emulated this feat.

Since 1991, he, like Kraftwerk, has been all but silent, as if realising he can no longer exceed himself.

If there was a difference between the rock guitar aesthetic of the late '80s and that of the early '80s, it was in the eyelids. Late '80s avant-rock, frazzled, psychedelia-tinged, "blissed out", as Simon Reynolds had it, lost in its own head, in the blizzards of its own rapture, was a heavy-eyelidded, concussed, oblivious affair, the soundtrack to an imaginary *Daydream Nation*, as Sonic Youth had it. This was music to nod out, to opt out to. Post-punk, by comparison, despite the acidic, incontinent sputtering of a Gang of Four's Andy Gill or a Keith Levene, was generally more vigilant, whether in its political outlook or towards its own workings, or the mechanisms of rock and the music industry as a whole. It was self-conscious, rather than on the edge of consciousness. The only "noise" equivalent of post-punk could be found in Public Enemy — Chuck D's nakedly combative and polemical rapping was driven home with sirens and alarms, most notably on the ascending, mutant squeal of *Rebel Without a Pause*. In the late '80s, hip-hop was still relatively marginal by later standards, yet to be hailed as pop's new lingua franca, but it brought the noise to a significantly widening audience and reconfigured the structure of the popular song. The impact of the likes of Eric B & Rakim in particular remains salutary, the more so since their approach has been abolished in many ways — Rakim celebrated his abilities as a wordsmith, while on the ultra-serrated likes of *Eric B Is on the Cut*, his DJ partner demonstrated to its fullest potential the scratch as a viable musical tool. Coupled with the neo-industrial blasts coming out from the continent (Neubauten, Switzerland's The Young Gods — who used samplers as a means of reanimating rock's dead tissue — and Front 242, among others), the late '80s felt like a time in which, from all sides, rock and pop's snivelling and decrepit orthodoxies were under siege from noise's cannon's roar.

As ever, it wasn't to be — so far, and no further. Nirvana carried the baton of rock as self-immolating noise the furthest, inheriting the sound and fury of Dinosaur Jr and The Pixies, but since

Kurt Cobain's 1994 demise, no one else has come close. With the exception of Radiohead's *Amnesiac*, a high profile dalliance with experimentalism, mainstream rock has reverted to so many retro amalgams. Hip-hop, meanwhile, once it took on a gangsta component, became more of a vehicle for self-aggrandising fantasy narratives, less concerned with exploring its own potential — by the mid-'90s, driven by an MTV-sponsored need for homogeneity, hip-hop had been reduced, sonically, to a dull fistful of tropes. Of course, there were, and are, many, many exceptions to that, from Busdriver to New Kingdom, but such artists paid a commercial price for innovation.

The other great noise of the late '80s was Acid House, whose Roland 303 signature synth squiggles and, soon-to-be-criminally repetitive, beats created a new generation gap in dance music — the ecstasy-induced Smiley culture, glowsticks and rattles all added grist to the Ian McDonald accusation of the "infantilising" effects of minimalism, for minimalist this music certainly was — artists like The Aphex Twin found himself being bracketed alongside Terry Riley and Steve Reich, of whom he had never heard. However, this music not only placed itself beyond society's pale in its illegitimacy, taking place outside the borders of licensing control, in fields, old hangars, squats, etc. — but in the very nature of the music, which refused to progress usefully, promote individual stars who might feed industry and boost our pop exports. Instead, it remained fixated pointedly and pointlessly upon its own moment of bliss.

Rave also helped disseminate ambient music, as the chill-outs that followed all-nighters became a zone in which beatless, lush soundscapes assisted comedown at the break of dawn — hence the likes of KLF and The Orb. This, in turn, revived interest in the music of Brian Eno, whose ambient projects in the late '70s were greeted as frivolously indulgent curios by rock critics of the day (as Eno himself notes with amusement), but which would turn out to be of far greater future significance than the thick-sideburned guitar legions to whom they devoted the greater part of their attention back then. Records like *Music for Films*, *Music for Airports* and *On Land* were some 15 years ahead of their time. And, while Eno's aims were supposedly an antidote to rock's would-be-rowdy subversiveness — to create a modern-day equivalent of Satie's proposal of a music that could take its humble place amid the clank of cutlery at the dining table — as Muzak it failed. As noted in Joseph Lanza's *Elevator Music*, when *Music for Airports* was played at an actual airport, there were complaints from travellers. For, though the music is, on the face of it, soothingly, luxuriantly tonal, its loops and repetitions, its innovation provoked a sense of disquiet, invited unwanted introspection among nervous fliers rather than the mild, familiar assurance of docility a Kenny G would have provided.

Eno's ambient albums were cerebral, deceptively tranquil and full of yearning, replete with what Nietzsche described as "nostalgia for the infinite", which sets it apart from the nostalgia for the '60s and '70s of most airport lounge music. His ideas were taken up widely in the '90s, as ambient came into its own as a genre rather than the mere quirk of an artsy ex-Roxy Musician. The results were variable and few came close to matching Eno's originals, in terms of both their strategic acuity and limpid beauty. At worst, they provided a mere slush of aural Radox or an accompaniment to spurious, New Age placebos.

Indeed, this would be the problem with the '90s across the board — the most untroubled decade of recent times. Of course, there was any amount of human misery and international strife.

However, in that period of economic fair weather, bracketed by the collapse of the Soviet Union and the blissfully unanticipated collapse of the Twin Towers, music tended to eschew the dissonant, the countercultural, the jagged and probing in favour of a certain high-quality luxury — even if this was the luxury of angst, as evinced by, say, Massive Attack and Portishead, whose disquieting elements did not prevent them from being coffee-table staples. Acid, rave, techno, ambient, all inadvertently bled into a pleasant, wine bar and coffee house tropicalia, found in the likes of Kinobe, Air and Amorphous Androgynous, among others. Hip-hop was no longer the Black CNN, nor the principles of Cage and collage extended into popular funk — despite the likes of Dre, Tupac and Snoop claiming to tell it how it was, their video fantasy worlds contained no white people, no agents of a wider racism, no acknowledgement of poverty but merely an anarchic Dogg-eat-dog ghetto world, an apolitical riot of bling and booty.

The great, modernistic giant steps of both contemporary classical and jazz music faltered somewhat in the late '60s, at around the same time. Since then, both have had to contend with dwindling market shares and a lengthy period in which their extreme innovations fell out of vogue, and during which both were in danger of becoming academic concerns, or, to paraphrase Miles Davis, the stuff of museums. However, with the rise of the CD format, the early '90s saw a vast slew of reissues of this longer-form music, which, for classical music in particular, had been hard to contain within the vinyl format. As well as the traditional staples of Bach, Beethoven, Mozart, this meant a reawakening of interest in twentieth-century classical music. However, it was not the urgently cryptic music of Boulez, Berio, Nono and Stockhausen which the CD-buying public feasted upon but the lugubrious, luxuriant, liturgical works of Arvo Pärt and John Tavener, or early music such the Abbess Hildegard of Bingen (whose *A Feather on the Breath of God* was sampled on rave/pop group The Beloved's *The Sun Rising*), and, most notable of all, Henryk Górecki's *Symphony No. 3*, which was a sizeable enough hit to make The South Bank Show sit up and take notice. This sort of success crossed over into the jazz world, via Jan Garbarek, whose *Officium*, recorded on ECM, was another surprise success, melding his own airborne, reverberant saxophone phraseology with The Hilliard Ensemble's renditions of choral music by Cristóbal De Morales, Pérotin and others. Despite the genuine merits and high intentions of much of this music and its undeniable gravitas (*Symphony No. 3* took the Holocaust as its subject matter), one also suspects that this music functioned as a sort of superior ambient, hallmarked with a certain cathedral authenticity. After a century of esoteric, secular, modernistic, "difficult" classical music, these records accorded with a vague hankering for spirituality and the formal, sepulchral simplicity of pre-modern times, which could be found in the opulent, sonorous drones of a Tavener or a Pärt. In place of the knotty over-development of a Boulez was tonality, repetition, a virtuous balm showering gently from some vaguely divined higher place. This was what one writer has described as "healing the wound" of the twentieth century, with all its violence and schisms and a similarly fractured music to match — an inadvertent soundtrack to materially better times and the historian Francis Fukuyama's *The End of History and the Last Man.* (In case this should sound like sneering on my part, I ought to confess that I bought into this music wholesale myself, availed of its comforts.)

For all its materiality and hedonistic tendencies, the music scene as a whole in the '90s was more active, more diverse, more multifarious, more fragmented and eclectic than it had ever been before, mainstream or otherwise — promiscuity between genres was rampant, genres themselves broke down into micro-genres, new technologies encouraged new musical mutations. It was more layered — Hendrix had caused a stir by using 8-track recording; now a group like Garbage were using 96 tracks. Movements like drum'n'bass were co-opted as signifiers of cool in TV soundtracks before they'd even had the chance to generate hit singles. The growing influence of world music, albeit in sanitised forms, as an object of interest in its own right or as an addition to Western music's spice rack, was palpable, as the music of past decades were plundered either for samples or simply for their own sake. However, rather than create the conditions for a more advanced tolerance, it created a confusion — the Britpop movement, Oasis and Blur in particular, bespoke a consumer desire for a return to '60s-type cultural conditions, and a single, white focal point for common discussion à la The Beatles — simpler, more consensual times. The science of marketing developed rapidly in the '90s at a far greater pace than the art of making genuinely new music, which, hindered by entropy, the burden of what had already been achieved and the lack of new, virgin territories to conquer, had developed only incrementally. These were the beginnings of the times we still live in today — in which experimental music, truly adventurous and modern, was no longer able to make inroads but market-forced to live and breed underground.

CHAPTER 6

ART WILL EAT ITSELF?

From the late '50s onwards, the visual arts moved beyond the merely modern, beyond the merely expressionistic, into the realms of the conceptual. This was the logical upshot of the detonations of the great art movements of the early twentieth century, which sought to collapse art's traditional privileges and bring it crashing down into the world. A few of those privileges, however, still remained — the primacy of the gallery, the containment of the picture frame, the location of the viewer in relation to the piece of art, as well as complacent assumptions about the inherent values a piece of art was supposed to transmit.

Conceptual art sought to dismantle these remaining assumptions. Conceptual art was not about the end product but the invisible idea that gave rise to it, and if this new art form was about exhibiting ideas, then that theoretically precluded the need for galleries and the middle-men such as dealers, sponsors and patrons whose grip conceptual art also looked to loosen. Artists like Lawrence Weiner and Robert Barry participated in installations, such as the one at Windham College, Vermont, in 1968 which were "site-specific". These pieces were commentaries on their physical situation, the materials, fixtures and fittings surrounding them. They were temporary — once the exhibition was over, they would be taken down, thereby scotching the myth of art's permanency, from which so much of its prestige derived.

Contraptions such as Xerox machines were embraced as key inventions, perhaps the ones which would usher Art into Benjamin's vaunted Age of Mechanical Reproduction. Marshall McLuhan, naively perhaps, had hailed the photocopier as the invention which would render issues of copyright and ownership obsolete, enable "instant stealing" and provide a radical new means of transmitting information. Weiner was among those who contributed to a "Xerox Book" (published, ironically, rather than Xeroxed) which aimed to scramble fixed ideas about authenticity and the Original.

Weiner took the principle of mechanical involvement in art still further, with his series of *Removal* paintings, which were produced with a spray gun and compressor, duly relegating to obsolescence the role of the artist as individual expressionist. The *Removal* works did not just alter the traditional role of the artist/producer, however, but also that of the consumer, who when receiving one of the *Removal* paintings would be allowed to make choices as to its size and colouring.

Again, the "creation" in the case of a project like *Removal* wasn't the works themselves but the idea to execute them in this manner. This idea of "secondary information" he took further in his work *Statements* which contained a series of "enunciations" cleverly expressed in past participles ("One quart exterior enamel thrown on a brick wall"), which, thus grammatically phrased, managed to function as both definite and suggestive at the same time.

Even the primacy of colour was challenged — mathematics, processes, permutations and the written word now become key components, both tracking and anticipating developments in the information age. Of course, the words in a work like Joseph Kosuth's *Art as Idea as Idea*, which consists of a photostatted dictionary definition, are not in themselves designed to convey information, but to signify it.

Robert Barry was another artist whose work was deliberately devoid of "ideal meaning". He had participated in the Windham College installation with a work that was visible only at night, when a luminous nylon chord delineated the space it occupied (indeed, the piece was so large that it was impossible to perceive in full from any one position). With 1967's *Untitled*, he moved still further away from the visual — what is important is not so much what you see but what you experience. Consisting of four small squares which blend into the background of the gallery wall, the piece initially feels like the visual art's equivalent of John Cage's *4'33"* — in other words, what one is looking at is the absence of a painting, as if to stress the impotency of art as it is traditionally understood.

Conceptual art was so bold in breaking every taboo, so bent on "dematerialising" that it teetered on the verge of dissolving art altogether. It also raised the question: how to sell this stuff? What exactly is for sale?

In *Conceptual Art and the Politics of Publicity*, Alexander Alberro explains the pivotal role of Manhattan dealer/entrepreneur Seth Siegelaub, who set up his first gallery in New York when only in his early twenties. Alberro was alive both to the saleability of modern art to corporations, who saw an association with the visual avant-garde as a means of affirming their own, dynamic, go-ahead status and the nouveau riche, for whom its hipness and, of course, expense affirmed their social standing. For all their anti-art idealism, all of the above artists elected to be marketed by Siegelaub. He spoke of his artist's desire to reach a "much larger public" as if their mission were solely evangelical, glossing over any possible financial motivation.

Siegelaub wasn't merely a crude huckster who knew how to flog a pile of bricks with an enormous price tag attached to some gullible sucker. Indeed, in order to do his job, he had to become a theorist and art essayist in his own right. It was even suggested that Siegelaub was so closely involved with his artists that he was an artist of sorts himself, though he always refuted this.

However, it did mean that when he was liaising with patrons, buyers, organising exhibitions, etc., he was much more effective in persuading them to part with money for intangible goods, to "rationalise the purchase", as Baudrillard put it. This he did using the "sell-the-sizzle-not-the-steak" techniques of Madison Avenue, to which he soon relocated his premises. Sometimes, the art and Siegelaub's publicity of the art merged. One Barry work, *Inert Gas Series/ Helium, Neon, Argon, Krypton, Xenon/ From a Measured Volume to Indefinite Expansion*, was presented to the public in the form of a poster, widely distributed by Siegelaub, which contained a photo of the Southern Californian landscape in which Barry had let loose various volumes of inert gas into the atmosphere. Of course, only the landscape was visible in the picture. Only Siegelaub's tersely descriptive blurb accompanying the poster constituted any evidence of its existence.

For Alberro, Siegelaub's most important role in art history was his drawing up the *Artist's Reserved Rights Transfer and Sale Agreement*, which, Alberro asserts, "unwittingly codified the overlap between capitalism and the arts." This arose following a disagreement between Panayiotis Vassilakis (aka Takis) and New York's Museum of Modern Art, over a piece of his they had replaced without his consultation. Takis had recently participated in the May 1968 protests and was still simmering with revolutionary fervour. He stormed into MOMA and took the offending work hostage. MOMA's management attempted to negotiate with him, but a much wider issue was at stake here — the right of the artist over his or her own work. He also raised the question of whether museums like MOMA, with their trustees drawn from some of America's biggest institutions and corporations, were really fit to exercise the powers to display (or withdraw) artworks, whether they could be "neutral". As a result, the Art Workers Coalition was formed, with a view to bypassing the traditional constrictions, conventions and demands of galleries, museums and collectors and achieving the true "democratisation" of the arts which was at the heart of the conceptualist project.

For a brief moment, the Art Workers Coalition appeared to represent a triumph of labour over capital, and Siegelaub appears to have been genuinely politicised as he sided with the artists. He drew up the Agreement after extensive consultation, one which all future owners of a work of art would be obliged to sign, one which laid particular stress on its Notice, which, he insisted, should always be attached to the work, or, if the work were immaterial, to a piece of documentation describing the work. This, Alberro argues, was the key step in enabling conceptual art to take its place in the market. "The aura absent in conceptual art was thereby reintroduced in the aurarization of the signature."

The conceptualists went to great pains to remove art's sacred props, in hopes of democratising whatever was left (if anything) once they had done so. But that signature, that tiny signature, was enough to preserve the vital notion of the arts as possessable, authentic, as investments both spiritual (ah, the aura, the invisible, irradiating hum of meaning) and, of course, economic. You could remove the paint, the canvas, the gallery, even the very material object ("The world is full of objects … I do not wish to add any more", said the artist Douglas Huebler in 1969). But what could not be removed was market value. There was a deep-seated desperation on the part of those for whom the purpose of wealth was to make purchases to signify their wealthiness, to buy something, anything, so long as it was incredibly expensive and so long as it was certifiably one-off, bona fide Art — a desperation which ultimately could not be denied. In 1972, Lucy Lippard wrote,

> It seemed in 1969 . . . that no one, not even a public greedy for novelty, would actually pay money, or much of it, for a xerox sheet referring to an event past or never directly perceived, a group of photographs documenting an ephemeral situation or condition, a project for work never to be completed, words spoken but not recorded; it seemed that these artists would therefore be forcibly freed from the tyranny of a commodity status and market-orientation. Three years later, the major

> conceptualists are selling work for substantial sums here and in Europe; they are represented by (and still more unexpected — showing in) the world's most prestigious galleries. Clearly, whatever minor revolutions in communication have been achieved by the process of dematerialising the object . . . art and artists in a capitalist society remain luxuries.

Says Dan Fox of *Frieze* magazine,

> That late '60s moment is a fascinating one because it's when the idea of modernism, all those utopian aspirations of the pre-war seem to have failed recognisably — the transcendence or universality of art, art as universally enjoyable, which dovetails with the utopian aspirations of May 1968, the idea that art can be part of revolutionary movements, have that utilitarian function — that artists should be out there in the street, doing things for the community.

One artist who entertained fewer qualms about this sort of thing was conceptual art's poster boy Andy "good business is the best art" Warhol. He mimicked the workings, in that disingenuous, deadpan way of his, of the consumer society which art presumed itself to be somehow located above and beyond, with his silkscreen printed artworks. His was not the one-man operation art was supposed to be — the heroic, individual outsider — rather, he set up a factory, of whose operations he was director, much as in the world of industry or commerce. He managed to have his Campbell's soup and drink it — on the one hand apparently embracing American consumerism and buying shamelessly into its market values, while at the same time maintaining a quite definite, saleable and altogether traditional artistic aura, as a Maker of Statements. One might take his art two ways — as a commentary on the infantile and ephemeral preoccupations of modern America and the pernicious potency of brands, or as a celebration, even a sanctification of icons like Taylor and Monroe, whose ultimate job, like a Princess Diana, is to do nothing but simply and eternally be themselves. Pay your money, take your choice. In the end, the market Warhol professed to adore took Warhol for what Rembrandt, Picasso, Klee and Pollock were before him — an Artist, whose works multiplied in value following his death. Just how speedily, one wonders, would Walter Benjamin be revolving in his grave at the irony of Hugh Grant's making a profit of many millions, selling a Warhol original whose purpose was to remark on the debunking of art in the age of mechanical reproduction?

Since the late nineteenth century, composers such as Scriabin dreamt, with a sort of faraway, alchemical fervour, of synaesthesia — a synthesis between music and the visual arts. For the remainder of the twentieth century, the two forms engaged with each other, envied each other and attempted to take on the properties of the other. Eventually, such a thing as sound art was mooted — a term first coined by Canadian composer Dan Lander in the 1980s. The definition begs many questions, and even some of its supposed proponents, such as Christian Marclay, find it unsatisfactory. Is sound that is art "sound art"? Or is sound art merely the audible dimension of a new strain of conceptual art? Is sound art compatible with either the traditional forms of dissemination, such as CDs, or, for that matter, the constraints of the art gallery, with their conventions of stasis and, if not silence, then certainly quietude? And what, finally, is the difference between music, great music, and sound art?

"I distinguish between 'music' and 'sound art' on philosophical grounds," says the writer and academic Christoph Cox. "That is, sound art is sonic art that draws attention to the conditions of possibility of sound and audition (what the philosopher Gilles Deleuze calls 'the virtual' or 'the transcendental' domain) while music takes these conditions for granted and proceeds to use sounds as they come (what Deleuze calls 'the actual'). So sound art is generally concerned with what lies at the limits of music — noise, silence, and everyday sound — while music tends simply to accept a set of sounds (generally, the chromatic scale) and to use these to produce audible structures that draw attention to themselves rather than their conditions of possibility." Cox sees sound art as similarly situated to conceptual art, in that it is about the experience rather than the object. One of the key tenets of sound art is that it be “site specific”, as well as specific in other aspects. Musicians like Phill Niblock and La Monte Young have expressed resentment at their music being issued on CD, since the format doesn’t does justice to the length of their works, nor can they set its volume, which they consider to be a key aspect of their sound designs.

There are practical difficulties with sound art. The quiet of the gallery is one, except in the improbable event that the installation’s sound has been set at a high decibel level. The ambient sounds of parties of schoolchildren charging up and down the corridors, the hum of central heating systems or the sharp patter of stiletto heels on wooden floorboards are all potential sources of disruption. Then, there is the problem of permanency. It is easy for a piece of plastic art to be installed, in its place, 24/7 in a gallery. For sound, this means setting up a tape loop, which is somehow aesthetically distressing, emphasising as it does the artifice of the thing and absence of a performer. It sends out the message this is meta-music, music at a remove. The artistic duo Juneau Projects, who also make music framed within the context of conceptual art, attempted to circumvent this problem by performing themselves, in a gallery in Lithuania, in what photographic evidence suggests was an uninhibited performance of guitar-driven gusto. However, this only had the effect of clearing the room — the complex taboos of the gallery cannot be dispensed with such airy disregard. What are you supposed to do when the artists are “playing” like that? Can you look them in the eye? Do you applaud? Are they there, as performers, or are they flesh and blood “artworks”?

Sound art in outdoor locations has the advantage of escaping the prescribed conditions and often inadequate curation of the gallery. There have certainly been some spectacular successes, such as Xenakis’s *Persepolis*, set among the ruins of Persepolis, in Iran, which would undoubtedly have been a healthy antidote to the crushingly banal sound and light shows set up for tourists in Egypt, around the Pyramids or temples of Luxor.

Furthermore, one can make more creative use of the natural sounds of the environment. Indeed, as John Cage would have endorsed, it is possible with outdoor installations to incorporate chance, non-musical elements into the realms of music itself. So, when sound artist David Dunn set up an oscillator tone in the middle of a forest, it triggered off a chain of responses from the woodland wildlife — thereby restoring a unity between the artifice of art and the actual, living world. A number of works, by so-called earthworks, or land artists, follow this tradition. Outdoor installations can make an impressive, and imaginative, use of scale — Faust once participated in a performance in which the players were set up hundreds of yards apart from one another, on hilltops, producing a sort of vast, stereophonic effect, while Alvin Curran's *Maritime Rites* was performed on a riverside barge outside the Tate in 2006 and incorporated the nearby bells of St Pauls, foghorns and a host of other sounds associated with the river. A sceptic could argue that since the invention of the Walkman, all music has the potential to be the soundtrack to wide-ranging locations — a Harold Budd album could be experienced over the course of a two mile walk across suitably open, Californian terrain. That is not quite the same, however. The music is still inside your head, literally so in the case of headphones. Outdoor installations take the music out of your head and put it back into the environment. The results are generally spectacular and inherently moving, like watching an old friendship publicly resumed.

Field recordings are sometimes classified as sound art — the sort of outdoor recordings in which Luc Ferrari and ex-Cabaret Voltaire member Chris Watson specialise. Insofar as they take as their subject matter the recorded stuff of the world, they are clearly a musique concrète. However, whereas Luc Ferrari's field recordings, for example, are processed and arranged, many field recordings are, in effect, aural snapshots — as carefully chosen and meticulously recorded as any photographic session, and, at best, with the same, beautiful results.

Such recordings cross an interesting line. First of all, they are, unlike even the most workaday piece of pop music, figurative rather than abstract. They represent objects, be they ice floes, rainforests, or chirruping crickets. Secondly, while not necessarily claiming that such sounds are music, they encourage in the listener the same attentiveness that they would apply to music. As F Murray Schafer wrote, "My approach [...] has been to treat the world as a huge macro-cosmic composition, which deserves to be listened to as attentively as a Mozart symphony." Again, Cage is central here, claiming that the sounds he would hear when walking in a park were as pleasing to him as any music, while David Toop is foremost among contemporary critics who are inclining away from music appreciation alone, towards an appreciation of the very act of listening — to make a claim for the neglected primacy of the ear.

Sound art, though it's been around for some decades, still feels nascent and crying out for further development and exposure. Because it is more of an experience than something you would "possess", it has yet to attain any significant market value — the advantage of which is it resists commodification. It has, however, enabled artists who might have languished in the obscure margins to cross a bridge into the more prestigious, visual realms. Mayo Thompson, Mike Kelley and Christian Marclay are among those who have found their reputations upgraded by involvement in the visual world, while Paul Schütze is a more recent example of someone who has used this particular junction to cross over from music into the visual arts, where he is more likely to enjoy the attention that was always his due, but less likely to come his way if he stuck to making music. Sound art has yet to succeed in achieving a parity of privilege between experimental music and experimental visual art. The white walls have yet to be laid low. But at least they are beginning to reverberate; as Christoph Cox writes, "In eschewing mass-media content, [sound art] proposes a more radical exploration of the formal conditions of the medium itself. Against the anaesthetic assault of daily life, it reclaims a basic function of art: the affirmation and extension of pure sensation."

CONCLUSION

Since Kandinsky and Schoenberg first became pen pals, music and art have been attempting to find common ground, common purpose. The relationships and crossovers between the two have been frequent and intense; the more so in the twenty-first century as sound, along with video, has become an increasingly common feature of the art gallery. And yet, for all this, the fortunes of the two avant-gardes remain polarised. A friend of mine recently waxed eloquently on the virtues of the abstract artist Patrick Heron, her favourite painter. She was quite at ease with the inter-relationship in his work between form, colour, space and expression, and would have scorned anyone who made the gaffe of suggesting his canvasses could be knocked up in 20 minutes with a tray of paint and a roller. I happened to have my iPod with me and selected a piece by AMM from 1966. I watched as, slowly, her furrowed frown transformed into a grimace before she plucked the headphones from her ears like two irritating lumps of wax. "It sounds like someone tuning up," she declared, and looked me up and down as if to suggest that I belonged in some sort of institution. I passed the iPod around the rest of the table, to the three or four people who moments earlier had been nodding appreciatively along to my friend's tribute to Heron. The result, and the verdict, was the same in each case. "It sounds like someone tuning up," followed by querying glances at my countenance for signs of latent maniacal tendencies.

Of course, such an impromptu experiment is a wholly unfair reflection on those who participated in it, and the results predictable. It is not that my friends were Philistines, far from it — rather, this was the first time that the artistic practices of an AMM had swum into their ken, and they were naturally bewildered. Why is this attitude so commonplace, so late on? Why has this music failed obdurately to make the same inroads that modern art has into the collective consciousness? Modern art is so totally dominated by avant-garde ideas that one almost has sympathy for the Stuckists, who complain that relatively orthodox modes of expression in the visual arts have been marginalised. Precisely the opposite situation prevails in music, where the orthodox holds dull sway. Why does the nonconformist, the unexpected, the dissonant, still upset modern listeners, when, as the popularity of the Tate Modern abundantly demonstrates, it is an imperative in the visual arts? Perhaps it's something to do with the following:

The Original

> This new status of the original work is the perfectly rational consequence of the new means of reproduction. But it is at this point that a process of mystification again enters. The meaning of the original work no longer lies in what it uniquely says but what it uniquely is. How is its unique existence evaluated and defined in our present culture? It is defined as an object whose value depends on its rarity. This value is affirmed and gauged by the price it fetches on the market. But because it is nevertheless a 'work of art' — and art is thought to be greater than commerce — its market price is said to be a reflection of its spiritual value. Yet the spiritual value of an object, as distinct from a message or an example, can only be explained in terms of magic or religion. And since in modern

> society neither of these is a living force, the art object, the 'work of art' is enveloped in an atmosphere of entirely bogus religiosity. — John Berger, *Ways of Seeing*, 1972.

The power of the visual arts resides to a discomfiting degree in the power of the Original. As we have seen, conceptual art's attempts to depart from this principle have been in vain. Despite Walter Benjamin's best hopes, the power of the Aura of the Original, the Authentic, is as potent in its grip as it is utter in its spuriousness. On 20 January 2008, the *Independent on Sunday* reported that two Bacons were to go up for sale at rival auction houses and expected to fetch over £50 million between them. The short report contained eight pound signs ("£25m", "£25m", "£35m", "£26.5m" "£25.m", a pulse-quickening "£180m", "£5m" and "£35m") but no allusion whatsoever to the paintings' aesthetic merits, except to remark, in the strapline, that the fabulous sums Bacon's work would fetch "puts the artist firmly among the greats". It was, however, illustrated with sizeable reproductions of the works in question. A week later, the *Sunday Telegraph* reported, "Graffiti Artwork To Fetch £5m".

Again, the brief report was a good deal longer on financial details than it was on artistic assessment. This was generously illustrated by the piece in question, *Palm Springs Jump* (1982) by Jean-Michel Basquiat and the further information that Basquiat died in 1988, aged 28, thereby, of course, helpfully boosting the value of the canvas still further, since there is nothing like death to add that vitally distressing finishing touch to Authenticity.

People cannot help it — they goggle at the Original. Crowds gather six rows deep around the bullet-proof glass casing containing the *Mona Lisa* at the Louvre, as if seduced by years of propaganda about the intrinsic and elevating properties of art, notions scotched by John Carey in his *What Good Are the Arts?* As well as a genuine desire to examine the painting and meditate on its qualities, one senses an underlying belief that to be close to the *Mona Lisa* will be to bask in the mysterious, spiritually nutritious rays emanating from its centuries-old, cracked paintwork, that magic touch of the immortal passed on by Mr da Vinci and transmitted via his works. This is the Aura — one can disbelieve in the Aura, but insofar as it exercises such an undeniable, magnetic effect, it exists. It is that which emanates from all objects sanctioned as works of art, including, regardless of his own intentions, Marcel Duchamp's readymades. To possess such a work is like, well, what is it like? — possessing one's own private wishing stone, or a sacred relic of the True Cross, or an authentic piece of Immortal Soul? Or perhaps it merely confirms that you are an extremely rich and, therefore, extremely important person.

Many of those who attend performances of classical music, opera in particular, in all probability do so in the hope of elevation, both spiritual and social. However, in music, there is no equivalent of the Original. There is some trade in memorabilia, though we are talking in sums of thousands rather than millions — from beer mats on which the lyrics for million-selling hit singles were scribbled to Hendrix's guitar. What motivates the people who buy such things — superstition, vanity — is hard to fathom. What does the person who buys John Lennon's white piano imagine they have in their possession?

Master tapes, however, simply do not have the same cachet as Originals in visual art. They are not displayed in galleries for your aural delectation. They do not go under the hammer at Sotheby's. There is egalitarianism in music which does not exist in art. When those who are not simply downloading all of their music for free enter the remaining High Street record shops, they find that the great stuff is priced at about the same as the rubbish. An artist's sales might increase if they die, but the price of their records does not multiply, because, they are just that: records, reproductions, with an extremely limited market value. Like any self-respecting music journalist — or self-loathing, for that matter — I have spent much of my life lovingly accumulating a collection of records, a bounteous universe of aesthetic delights spanning the genres and the centuries, which even were I to live eight times over, devoting my every waking minute exclusively to record playing, I would not be able to attend properly to. Were I to sell that collection, I would probably only raise enough for a down payment on some middling piece of work by a first-time, straight-out-of-art-school exhibitor. Yes, there is some trade in rarities, but even then, the amounts are relatively piddling.

To boost the value of a music "original" to arthouse levels is practically impossible. The musician, writer and academic David Toop recalls trying to set up a concert at the Lisson Gallery in Marylebone, whose name puns with poignant irony. The owner of the gallery was enthusiastic, but wondered if there was a way in which the musicians could get paid the sort of sums a visual artist might expect for a similar installation.

"He wondered if the concert could be recorded, and then the recording sold immediately afterwards? I said to him, 'Well, you could try!' Over there on my desk is a CD-R of a concert I played a few days ago, of which only three copies exist in the world. But I couldn't give it away. If I were to try and sell it to Mark Wastell (who runs the Sound 323 record shop in Highgate), he probably wouldn't take it off my hands — and he was involved in the concert!

"The art and property boom have gone hand in hand since the 1980s," continues Toop. "That's when I think there was a wider realisation that to own a piece of art was both cool and a potential investment. Meanwhile, music gets cheaper and cheaper — down to less than a pound for a single track on mp3."

The composer La Monte Young has not only attempted to exceed the temporal conventions of music, with pieces with his Theatre of Eternal Music and other ongoing works — he also attempted to attain the status of his colleagues in the visual art world by withdrawing from the music marketplace in the early '70s and rendering himself and his soundworks as costly as a visual artist, relying on old-fashioned patronage. In 1974, he did manage to sell a piano, the centrepiece of a site-specific installation entitled *The Well-Tuned Piano* — the buyer even threw in an extra £1000 when Young autographed the thing for him. In general, however, buyers were insufficiently prepared to pay arthouse prices for any piece of music, no matter what connotations of originality and exclusivity you tried to dress it up in.

Sound artists like Michael J Schumacher have occasionally managed to sell on pieces of theirs, but it has been impossible to impinge on the relatively democratic nature of music's economy and dissemination.

Fascination with seven- and eight-figure sums and auction houses has had a tremendous knock-on effect for modern art. The sort of commonplace newspaper reports I quoted earlier have two effects: they appeal to people's avariciousness while also serving to expose the artworks — reproduced, yes, in miniature, yes — to a wider audience, helping the latter genuinely engage with "difficult" art and become more accustomed to the ideas it posits, as well as boost its cachet. Modern music has enjoyed no such privilege.

The Distress

Originally, this book was going to be called "abstract art versus abstract music", after a blog entry I wrote in 2004. Of course, those rashly penned terms are misleading. "Abstract" is just one of the branches of modern art, while all music is "abstract", i.e. non-representational. Perhaps the real equivalent for a Rothko is not Stockhausen but an Elgar or a Vaughan Williams, whose symphonic, wistful arcs are like great brushstrokes of colour, pregnant with meaning and ineffable expression. Perhaps modern art, even at its most harrowing, does not possess the capacity to traumatise the way music does. It's a truism but true nonetheless — we can close our eyes, but we cannot close our ears. Stanley Kubrick regularly raided the archives of "difficult" twentieth-century classical music when looking to soundtrack moments of high terror or anxiety in his movies, splicing together Bartok and Ligeti, for example, in the final sequences of *The Shining*. Picasso's *Guernica*, an unflinching depiction of the enormity of war, works across a large canvas but isn't so large as to be circumambient. It can be contained within a field of vision, it is static, it can be approached and, after perhaps a few minutes of sober rumination, walked away from.

The same is true of a Rothko. His art is an attempt to immerse the viewer, but, despite heavy promptings, such as the dim lighting of the Rothko Room, there is a limit to the distress he can evoke — the limits of the canvas, of the rooms in which his canvasses are situated. Without attempting to determine which the "better" of the two is, it can be said that the Rothko Room is an easier prospect for the dilettante, the faint heart, or the sort of pretentious individual who wishes for some sort of self-validation by placing themselves in proximity to works of art for so long as they can bear it. Put bluntly, you can be in and out of there in six minutes, be in the café in a further five. Exposure to Stockhausen's *Hymnen* means a commitment, in a darkened concert hall, for the larger portion of two hours. If you're simply attending one of his performances for the kudos you imagine it will confer on you, you're in for a tough time, and may well decide, after 15 minutes, the game isn't worth the candle, in the unlikely event that you could be induced to attend at all.

Conceptual art did attempt to stretch the temporal limits of the visual arts — Andy Warhol's several-hour-long film of the Empire State Building, for example, which, arguably, required a far greater tolerance than any piece of avant-garde music (but this felt like a gesture rather than an incipient genre.)

In its most extreme manifestations, modern music can feel like an infliction, and a deliberate, searing one at that. Some of contemporary classical music's critics regard serialism, musique concrète and all its brutalist, misshapen offspring as a reflection of a century particularly scarred with extreme acts of violence. This is music whose crashing dissonance should be dispensed with, in order that a "healing" process can begin and as a symbolic means, perhaps, of abolishing atrocity itself. With remarks he made in interviews, Stockhausen implanted, inadvertently or otherwise, a connection between his music and apocalyptic events. Speaking to the journalist Jonathan Cott in the late '70s, he spoke of the impending end of the twentieth century and the beginning of the twenty-first as times in which the planet would be purged by cataclysms. "We have to go through these crises at the end of this century and during the first decades of the next, there is no other way," he declared, with finality. He certainly succeeded in implanting terror in the mind of one impressionable 15-year-old, who listened to the infinitely descending arcs of electronics which stalk the charred, depopulated, final "region" of *Hymnen* with a mixture of rapture and dread. Come the actual beginning of the twenty-first century and his prophesies found a fulfilment of sorts in the events of September 11, which he was reported to have described as a magnificent work of art, though he denied having said — or at least meant — any such thing.

Another advantage or perhaps curse of contemporary music is that its capacity to evoke the future is so much more potent than that of the visual arts. Even futurist art (unless you count St Elia's blueprints for the futuristic cities to come) deals in the stuff of its present day, albeit dynamically represented. It was up to speed but no further. Attempts to evoke What the Future Will Be Like tend to be banal, figurative affairs, the stuff of science fiction paperback covers and hardly within the rarefied realms of modern art at all. Futurism is evoked far more potently within the "blind" medium of music, offering at its best beguiling, sometimes disconcerting intimations of what might lie around the corner, heard but as yet unseen. This might be the fluid and shapeshifting, uncertain signals of music like Webern's, which slip the presets of traditional sound patterns, or the more rigid "New Sonic Architecture" of avant-rock groups like The Young Gods and Einstürzende Neubauten, which prompt the listener to paint their own mental pictures. This is not always congenial. What with 40 years of Cold War, and now the bleak prognoses of global warming, it is a long time since the future has felt like a place one would be inclined to dwell upon. Music, of course, is equally powerful in evoking a sense of the past, be it the "nostalgia for the infinite" in Eno's ambient music, or the simpler, Proustian pleasures of endlessly revived jukebox pop music and its perma-evocations of summers long ago. Given the choice of which way to face through time, it's clear to see why the après-garde direction is the more attractive option.

Again, however, this is not necessarily the case for Black music. For Black people as a whole, the past is likely to represent in large part pain, the future the possibility, at least, of improved circumstances. Hence, as we have seen, from dub pioneers like Lee "Scratch" Perry to jazz's great procession of innovators, from Louis Armstrong to the ultra-visions of Sun Ra (*Disco 3000*), from George Clinton and his "nigga in a spaceship" future funk, Black music has never been overly weighed down by any great wistful retrospection. What's more, a fascination with the supposed Otherness of Black music has meant that its inventions, which have often filled in historically where white music has fallen short, have gained wider exposure. It's hard to conceive that Duke Ellington's music was once considered "dissonant", or to recapture just what a fissure the joyful peal of Louis Armstrong's trumpet represented, breaking the ice of the twentieth century.

David Toop believes that people in general are inherently more tolerant of visual than of musical chaos. "I've thought about this cliché that we're a visually oriented society, that we're less sound oriented, but is that really true? Do we really prioritise the visual? I've been thinking about this in relationship to what David Hockney's been saying, that no one knows how to 'look' any more, that we have headphones and so forth ... It's about how we regard the senses. We think of them as discrete, but they're not. We can't regard them in isolation; what we think important isn't necessarily what is important at a more unconscious level. So hearing is actually very important to people, but they think that seeing is more important. And hearing is regarded as a secondary sense, alongside touch and smell, with seeing as the primary sense. But I'm not so sure. I think one of the things about music, about sound, is that it has a tremendous impact on people. We can put up with far more crap visually. You walk into Heathrow Airport, for example. It's a visual nightmare, but people aren't that troubled by it. You create an aural equivalent of that, and people would run screaming for the exits — which isn't to say the world isn't full of noise, because it is — but the world is also full of excruciating visual content."

Toop deplores the tendency of one or two noise practitioners to exploit music's potential to distress, whether merely to *épater le bourgeoisie* or as a demonstration of machismo, of hardcore credentials, as if noise music isn't an aesthetic instrument but a sonic equivalent of seeing who can hold their hand in the flame the longest, who can "take it". Critics can point to the apparent male domination of noise music in all its manifestations and ascribe the whole phenomenon to some sort as the product of dysfunctional maleness, a black scrawl of misanthropy, at worse, misogyny — Marinetti's "scorn for women" writ large in the sound field.

However, one of the more remarkable aspects of the supposedly esoteric, hermetic world of engineers, eccentrics and obsessives that constitute the avant-garde and experimental musical worlds is just how many women are actively engaged within it, and have been for many decades, and not merely in the performance or decorative roles too often ascribed them in other genres. There is Elisabeth Lutyens, who endured much derision, but eventually vindication, for her neo-Schoenbergian compositions. Daphne Oram and the late Delia Derbyshire, whose work with the BBC Radiophonic Workshop was only belatedly recognised, who were responsible for discreetly smuggling musique concrète into millions of households, not least in Derbyshire's arrangement of the Dr Who theme. Pauline Oliveros, electronic composer and Deep Listening advocate, who was still active in her seventies. A perfunctory swirl of the iPod wheel reveals a further host of names, spanning from rock to jazz, and making up just a small sample of a female involvement which amounts to a great deal more than a token presence. Alice Coltrane, Barbara Morgenstern, AGF, Natasha Barrett, Honey Owens, Carla Bozulich, Björk, Susanne Brokesch, Zeena Parkins, Janet Feder, Maja Ratkje, Colleen, Kevin Blechdom, Éliane Radigue, Gail Priest, Juana Molina, Mira Calix. Patty Waters, Tujiko Noriko. There is a particularly strong representation in electronic composition —

without venturing into some dubious theory about the amorphous, enwombing nature of electronica being somehow more "feminine", perhaps part of the reason for this is that this music does not require women to strike a pose — it's more meritocratic. As Peter Rehberg said, "I think the nature of electronic music is very liberating, you can do whatever you want — whereas in other genres there is machoism about it — you've got to 'be' in a certain world, Rolling Stones world — and if you have a 'lady' in your band it must be some sort of statement. Electronic music is largely instrumental; it isn't putting out messages in that sort of way."

What is considered distressing about modern music to some isn't the tyranny it attempts to impose, but the very opposite — its openness, its erasure of boundaries and outmoded, arbitrary strictures and hierarchies. Some find this freedom disorienting, but for many others, it represents the infinity of opportunity.

It is possible that a distrust of surprise, of noise, or its equally discomfiting corollary, silence, in music is intrinsic, deeply ingrained in the human psyche and goes back to our hunter-gatherer days, when any unexpected sound of unknown origin — the snap of a twig to your rear in the forest, for example — signalled mortal danger of some sort. However, it is more likely to be about custom — people aren't used to this stuff and, Catch-22, because they're unused to it, never get to be used to it. World music throws up some good examples here, especially that which emanates from less expansive, progressively bent cultures than our own. Take gagaku music, for example, which has been performed at the Imperial Court for several centuries. When it was first exposed to Western ears, it was considered unbearably dissonant (despite the word "gagaku" meaning "elegant") — the equivalent of that tiny dollop of green sauce served in Japanese restaurants which you are advised not to eat in amounts of more than a few molecules at a time. Post-war, gagaku had to be considerably diluted before being presented to Western audiences. However, it should also be observed that Japanese audiences, quite accustomed to gagaku, found Western classical music confusing and ugly. The Japanese, however, took the trouble to accustom themselves to it, and today there are numerous Japanese performers of Western classical music, even composers. This has not been a reciprocal embrace, however. As David Toop notes in *Ocean of Sound*, in 1990, there was an advert for Nurofen, the pain relief tablet. The symptoms of headache were soundtracked by a piece of gagaku. The symptoms of headache relief were sound tracked by *Étude*, by Mike Oldfield, taken from his somewhat anodyne soundtrack to the film *The Killing Fields*.

The words of the Japanese noise musician Merzbow seem apt here. "If noise means uncomfortable sound, then most pop music is noise to me."

The Corporation

The Doris Salcedo piece *Shibboleth* ostensibly invites meditation on the brutality of colonialism and the "stand-off between rich and poor". It is also sponsored by the global corporation Unilever. In January 2008, *Private Eye* included the following piece of cant from Unilever's Group Chief Executive, Patrick Cescau, reflecting on his company's sponsorship of the piece in their Pseud's corporate section. "This year we are delighted to welcome Doris Salcedo whose installation, Shibboleth, continues the tradition of innovation and experimentation established by previous artists in the Unilever series. Like all great artists, Salcedo invites us to see the world differently. She asks us to reflect on the boundaries, physical and emotional, that divide us as human beings. This is an exploration that resonates within Unilever. Understanding patterns of human behaviour is vital to a company that strives to meet consumers' everyday needs with products that make people feel good, look good and get more out of life."

So established is the supportive role of corporate sponsorship that it would probably be considered facile, even puerile, to query how a work of art supposedly protesting the global poverty gap could dovetail so neatly with the aspirations of a vast, profit-making concern like Unilever. It would be considered rude and inappropriate to wonder aloud whether Ms Salcedo herself agrees heartily with Mr Cescau and, in addition, exempts her patrons from any role in the hideous economic schisms which blight life on this earth and which her art seeks to highlight. Perhaps the idea is that this sponsorship deal is a compromise which could yet work in Ms Salcedo's favour — the exposure afforded her by Unilever will allow her art to demonstrate the nature of global injustice to a wider audience, which will shed light and sow seeds in the mind of the populace, and provide the first inklings of a dawning global consciousness, economically egalitarian in nature, which will serve to rein in dramatically the overweening dominance of corporations such as Unilever, who will thereby have served as agents of their own reduction. If we take this long view, discretion is important in the short term — therefore, best not highlight at all at this stage the sequential chain that exists between the Tate itself, re-branded today as providing the nation with its modern art treasures, and the ownership of slaves upon which Tate's fortune was originally based. High art has successfully laundered the Tate name.

It is perhaps more likely that corporations, or other commercial agencies, such as the property developers currently sponsoring Damien Hirst, know perfectly well what they are buying into when they buy into modern art. Back in 1969, the President of Philip Morris Europe, the big tobacco company, made the following declaration in regard to an art exhibition they were sponsoring entitled When Attitude Becomes Form. "We at Philip Morris feel it is appropriate that we participate in bringing these works to the attention of the public, for there is a key element in this 'new art' which has its counterpart in the business world. That element is innovation — without which it would be impossible to make progress in any segment of society [...] our constant search for a new and better way in which to perform and produce is akin to the questionings of the artists whose works are represented here."

These remarks do highlight a comparison between the processes of capitalism, its never-stand-still quest for new means and new modes of production, and the equivalent processes in the avant-garde that writers like myself are so wont to extol. It's a comparison that could potentially be as awkward for music as it is for the arts. However, it is the visual arts, whose radical innovations have now become so familiar to mass audiences as to be practically decorative, which have been far more effortlessly assimilated, with the minimum of distress. Modern art, or at least a certain portion of it, pre-exists in the realm of the "high", the same realm as high fashion, high society, high finance. It makes for an easy corporate bedfellow. Moreover, Salcedo's utopian protestations do not cause any discomfort to her sponsors — indeed, they are vital. As Mark Achbar, Jennifer Abbott and Joel Bakan so entertainingly, methodically and comprehensively demonstrate in their film *The Corporation*, big business is intrinsically psychopathic, even if those who serve to further its ends, even at the highest level, are themselves not. Modern art's ghostly aura of utopianism is just one of the many strategies corporations use to deodorise the inevitable stench of its ruthlessness. It's of a piece with Unilever's own homepage, which is decked with photos of happy, healthy children romping on hillsides, or its mission statement — "to add vitality to life".

The same sort of relationship does not exist with avant-garde music. Even if its soul were for sale, there are few buyers. In 1977, in his famous essay *Noise: The Political Economy of Music*, Jacques Attali argued that music, with which he equated "noise", was more integral to society than perhaps we would care to acknowledge — all the more reason for it to be kept on the peripheries when it moves faster than the political and economic tide. "More than colours and forms, it is sounds and their arrangements that fashion societies [...] All music, any organisation of sounds is, then, a tool for the creation or consolidation of a community, of a totality." Hence, the totalitarian's mistrust of "subversive noise". They, the theorists of totalitarianism, have "all explained, indistinctly, that it is necessary to ban subversive noise because it betokens demands for cultural autonomy, support for differences or marginality: a concern for maintaining tonalism, the primacy of melody, a distrust of new languages, codes, or instruments, a refusal of the abnormal — these characteristics are common to regimes of that nature..." Hence, so far, and no further.

Modern capitalism is more subtle than the totalitarians. Both the Nazis and, eventually, the Communist state in Soviet Russia banished and decried modern art. The Corporation has been able to embrace it and use it to its own ends. It has not, however, extended the same hand to equivalently modern music. It does not need to crush it with an iron fist, as the Czech authorities attempted to do to the tacitly dissident free rock group Plastic People of the Universe in the 1970s. But, by unconscious conspiracy and creeping risk aversion, it has been successfully pushed to the peripheries. A thousand cuts, from Arts Council decisions to playlist compilers to magazine editors, have kept it at bay.

Another Corporation, the British Broadcasting variety, was, however, a good deal more accommodating towards avant-garde music. In its radio infancy, the BBC took it upon itself to bring to listeners a regular repertoire of new music, particularly Schoenberg and the works of the Second Viennese School. Edward Clark, a former pupil of Schoenberg who worked at the BBC, was central to this initiative, which was sustained for some 14 years, between 1922 and 1936, when Edwards resigned from the BBC. Lord Reith, the austere but conscientious founder of the BBC, felt that radio listeners would be able to take on board new musical works, particularly those of an elevating and educative nature, with "comparatively little effort", particularly if they were presented under the guise of entertainment. The BBC were prepared to be quite bold in their broadcasting policy, making a point of including "futurist" or "art music", as they termed it. Not just the Viennese School, but Varèse, Poulenc and Honnegger were among the beneficiaries of this policy, as well as a number of contemporary British composers.

Listeners proved a little recalcitrant in the face of this highbrow policy. Rather than capitulate, however, the BBC decided that the problem was that their audience was listening improperly. And so, in 1930, in the *Radio Times*, they printed up a set of instructions, in bold upper case and pinstripe prose, detailing the procedure for what it termed "good listening". They included the following:

> CHOOSE YOUR PROGRAMMES AS CAREFULLY AS YOU CHOOSE WHICH THEATRE TO GO TO. IT IS JUST AS IMPORTANT TO ENJOY YOURSELF IN THE HOME AS IN THE THEATRE.
>
> LISTEN AS CAREFULLY AT HOME AS YOU DO IN A THEATRE OR CONCERT HALL. YOU CAN'T GET THE BEST OUT OF A PROGRAMME IF YOUR MIND IS WANDERING, OR IF YOU ARE PLAYING BRIDGE OR READING. GIVE IT YOUR FULL ATTENTION. TRY TURNING OUT THE LIGHTS SO THAT YOUR EYE IS NOT CAUGHT BY FAMILIAR OBJECTS IN THE ROOM. YOUR IMAGINATION WILL BE TWICE AS VIVID.

Listeners, however, were slow to knuckle down to these instructions and found themselves harangued in a later edition of the *Radio Times* by one Filson Young, who wrote: "Many of you have not even begun to master the art of listening; you have not even begun to try." Even charming blandishments such as these failed to persuade listeners, who kept up a steady murmur of disgruntlement at the nutritious, but to their tastes, less-than-delicious diet of modern music they were being served. One correspondent, Eric Lewis, remarked, "If Bartok, Stravinsky and co were administered in somewhat smaller doses, it might be possible to persuade the patient to keep them down. The 'treatment' so far has been rather too drastic."

The BBC continued to plead with listeners to rack that "conservative member" of theirs, the ear. The BBC Music critic Ernest Newman attempted to appeal to the British sense of fair play when attending to the new music. "You are not playing the game unless you hear it at any rate once," he urged. However, it was the *Daily Mail* who, couching their review in a tasteful military metaphor, derided a Schoenberg performance as a Teutonic phenomenon unsuited to the plain ears of John Bull.

"Not all who had thought they could stand an evening of Schoenberg held fast. A bold front was put up during the first part of the programme, but the British line wavered in the course of 'Pierrot Lunaire'. At one moment, the deserters were so many that it looked as though we were in a general retreat [...] Schoenberg's music is, outside Central Europe, incomprehensible. It belongs to countries where people are overdone and fed up with normal music. Outside Berlin and Vienna this art is meaningless, and the subtle Schoenberg a bore." The resistance held.

It's comical, of course, to contemplate the naivety of early broadcasters and their attempts to mould the musical tastes of a populace for whom life was arguably onerous enough without having to grapple with the rigours of serialism (though is the spectacle of their twenty-first-century equivalents — grown men and women with degrees and wardrobes full of sober suits, straightfacedly devising action plans and working within an internal marketing format towards the dissemination of dynamically generated content in a synergetic media environment — elaborate, jargon-addled systems out of whose final chute plops a re-commissioning of, tarantara, yet another Saturday night *Celebrities on Ice* extravaganza?). If this book amounts, in part, to an exhortation to a wider audience to attend more actively to avant-garde music, does it not raise the questions: Haven't people troubles enough on their plate already? Better things to do? There was a time when, with greenly ardent idealism, I entertained the notion that the music of, for example, Stockhausen, could appeal to the "masses", if only a hidebound and commercially self-interested media did not prevent them from hearing his work, afraid that it would liberate their minds from pap and trivia, shatter the glass cage from within which they regarded the Spectacle with passive docility, and so forth. I was at Oxford at the time and, during one holiday period, had had to leave the bulk of my record collection in a large trunk in the care of a fellow student who resided in a room opposite in our halls of residence and was remaining in college for the vacation. We had "scouts" as they were known, local ladies charged with the Augean task of cleaning up after first-year students whose views on the Bigger Picture may have been confidently fixed but whose grasp of the rudiments of domestic hygiene was less certain. Our scout was a pleasant, middle-aged lady called Pam. I had delivered, in the college bar, a sermon to the effect that Pam was precisely the sort of person whose hitherto undernourished soul might benefit from hearing some of Karlheinz's greatest hits — that the experience would prove to be an epiphany in her cultural life, one she'd been denied by commercial radio and TV's limited diet of banality. Imagine my elation then, when shortly after my return to college Pam remarked offhandedly to me as she emptied a waste paper bin that my friend had played her something by Stockhausen and she'd really, really enjoyed it. Bursting with vindication, I at once rushed across the corridor and hammered on my fellow student's door, to share with her what I'd just heard from the very lips of the working classes themselves. I did so — only to discover that my friend had put Pam up to affecting a deep appreciation of the works of Stockhausen. The whole thing was a wind-up, and I slunk away, the sound of Philistine cackling ringing in my ears, my evangelical ardour doused, once and forever, in derision.

Then again, the problem with those who evangelise for the arts in general is that they sometimes do so in terms that promote them as functional, utilitarian. The idea is a religious compound of guilt and the work ethic, and one into which people continue to buy at a subconscious level, even if they have consciously rejected it. The arts must be morally improving — you must come out of them a marginally better person than you entered them. A little more educated, a little more spiritually uplifted, a little fitter for life's purpose. If the arts don't engender any of these things, well, that is okay, so long as they provide some form of entertainment, for it is important to let one's hair down, the better to bundle it up again in the morning — or perhaps to soothe, to relax, so as to prevent the citizen from stress or burnout.

Both avant-garde music and avant-garde art can be problematic when it comes to function. So often, they appear neither to entertain nor to contain any obvious moral. They are, rather, quite gratuitous. What are they for? In the case of avant-garde art, armies of catalogue writers are commandeered to assure visitors of the political component intended by the creator of *Shibboleth*, even if it is hardly self-evident. Elsewhere, curious arrangements of lines, shapes and colours, or odd juxtapositions of objects, are, we are told, in that much-used old throwback, invitations to contemplate the spatial relationship between ourselves and things, the things and other things and the space they occupy. These, combined with the sepulchral hush and do-not-touch, forbidding stillness of the gallery, allow us to withdraw, after a few short minutes well spent, feeling duly wiser and less spatially complacent.

Once again, avant-garde music is less advantaged in this respect. Contemporary popular music criticism very often favours the text and therefore the more traditional grand narrative of the singer, the songwriter, writer of Great Songs, and working un-indulgently within the parameters of received, four square templates, or lightly armed with an acoustic guitar. Bob Dylan, in his time, has been the most conspicuous victim/beneficiary of this line of thinking. The literary critic Christopher Hicks stooped to study Dylan since, as a lyricist of great profundity, he qualified as honorary English Literature. Conversely, when Dylan dared to boost his sonic armoury by switching to electric guitar, it was as if he had violated some sacred, agrarian tenet. Dylan is a lot more playful than his admirers are comfortable with sometimes, while there is more to attend to in his music than just his lyrics. However, he is an example of the equation, often self-imposed, of political virtue and austere plainsong, one that has been repeated down the line, from Cornelius Cardew to Billy Bragg. To value texture over text (as, ironically, many of our most eloquent music critics, including Simon Reynolds and David Toop, do) is to be guilty of overindulgence, materialism — gratuitousness.

In fact, a great deal of avant-garde music does have value, purpose, content, meaning and function — often in the places where you least expect to find it. Throbbing Gristle, for example, do arguably have an ethical dimension. The deconditioning you experience on exposure to them is intended as beneficial. Free improv does provide a metaphor for a Greater Society, a paradigm of free expression and egalitarian interaction. The challenges set by modern music do require the virtue of tolerance in the listener, openness to alternative ideas and other cultures, and a mistrust of hierarchy for its own sake, which could form the basis of sound political thinking. But these are neither essential components to the music, nor can they be guaranteed to purge the listener of human deficiency. It takes a certain kind of courage, perhaps (or more likely, a unique strain of misanthropic moroseness) to clear a student disco by playing Sun Ra, as this writer did in his more callow days, but listening to *The Solar-Myth Approach (Vol. 1)* is not going to make you more likely to be the person who returns into a burning building to rescue a trapped child. The myth of the arts — any of the arts — as improving should have been scotched long ago, if only as recently when the high cultural habits of many concentration camp guards were revealed: Bach, Thomas Mann. Never mind no more poetry after the Holocaust, how about no more nonsense about its inevitable, improving effects?

The past 20 years have seen corporations, who pride themselves on associating with leading-edge innovations in the modern arts they sponsor, be rather more cautious when it comes the marketing of their products — music, in particular. The science of marketing has become more exact, with marketing departments now assuming a more creative role, which has encouraged a culture of risk aversion. In both promotion and publishing, the emphasis, more than ever, is on tried-and-trusted formulae and a small handful of trusted Giants of Rock, who, ironically, might never have emerged had they had the misfortune to have to navigate their way through today's adverse conditions.

Consequently, the relationship between the musical mainstream and its peripheries resembles the parted Red Sea. You can walk right down the middle of it and it feels like parched terrain — nothing there but the old, dead hulks of yesteryear on the seabed. Meanwhile, on either bank, it's straining and awash with activity, prevented from making it to the middle by some invisible force field.

Nowadays, what is great in music must be actively sought out. It will not be televised. While the rock narrative has faltered since the death of Kurt Cobain — in which its hallowed past has become fatally embalmed, even in the work of rock bands yet unborn — the spirit of guitar adventure still prevails: in the frantic, rearranged work of Wolf Eyes and Sightings, the immersive, deconsecrated Metal of Sun O))), in the vast, cinematic acreage of post-rock collectives like A Silver Mt. Zion, to name but a tiny few.

Crossovers of all kinds abound. Towards the end of his life, Steve Lacy was one of a number of jazz artists who were juxtaposing their playing with live electronics on recordings such as *New Jazz Meeting Baden-Baden 2002*. "Electronics" has crumbled and atomised into a fascinating bombardment of sub-genres, as new technologies find new ways of splitting what was hitherto considered un-splittable in sound. Artists like Fennesz, turntablist Philip Jeck and the Raster-Noton label work in a new medium of the tiniest particles, grains and glitches, their work often surging with poignancy and decay, yet crackling defiantly with life as the light fades elsewhere — decaying and abiding, like Gavin Bryars's *The Sinking of the Titanic*, an ongoing work about an ocean liner, representative of the hopes of twentieth-century modernity, sunk long ago. Dub has been imported from Jamaica into rock, techno, funk, adding what David Toop describes as "depth illusion" to music — practically a visual dimension. When the French author Jacques Lusseyran was struck blind, he wrote about his new relationship with sound. "Most surprising was the discovery that sounds never came from one point in place and never retreated into themselves. There was the sound, its echo and another sound into which the first sound melted and to which it had given birth, altogether an endless procession of sounds." He could be describing dub as experienced by the sighted.

As old rivers dry up, new tributaries erupt. The peripheries are where it is at, a promiscuous riot of cross-fertilisation. The macro is dead; long live the micro. It is too much to expect the giant strides of the '50s, '60s, '70s anymore, and that is a source of dismay to some, who long for the detonatory impact of the Great twentieth-century Movements, geyser-like eruptions of boiling foment from the underground. That will happen no more — such activity is now extinct.

What did happen, a few years ago, around the turn of the new millennium, as it coincidentally turns out, is that we finally arrived in the future. We've been in it for several years now. We've arrived. And this is what it's like. This book could as easily consist of an A–Z directory of the artists active over the last 20 years worthy of your attention, undeterred by zero commercial prospects, all of whose exclusion from this text represents a scandal (where the hell is Alvin Lucier? Keiji Haino? You mention Psychedelic Horseshit and fail to mention Silver Apples?) It's confusion worth embracing, rather than fleeing back into the teenage conformism of the latter-day *NME*.

A few years ago, someone from *The Wire* sent Stockhausen a number of new techno releases for his consideration. His responses ("I heard the piece Aphex Twin of Richard James carefully," and "I know that he [Plastikman] wants to have a special effect in dancing bars, or wherever it is.") hilariously reflected his absolute aloofness and disdain for an electrified music scene for which he laid the groundwork, and one could sympathise with him to a small degree — the idea that mainstream dance artists have made tonal "sense" of electronic music is not necessarily what he had in mind when he started out — some sort of total, spiritual metamorphosis of modern society was more along the lines of what he had been hoping for. Conversely, The Aphex Twin for many years had absolutely no knowledge of the sort of precedents critics were citing in reviews of his work — he had worked, blindly, as a teenager in Cornwall, with video games rather than musique concrète as his guide. That was then. Today, old hierarchies are collapsing; old genres are collapsing into one another. Magazines like *The Wire*, festivals in Europe, throw up fresh juxtapositions every month. In Brussels in March 2008, Sun Ra Arkestra saxophonist Marshall Allen and musique concrète composer Henri Pousseur rubbed shoulders on a bill that also included Ceramic Hobs and Psychedelic Horseshit. There is a new, meerkat awareness of what everyone else is doing. A great many more dialogues have been taking place between hip-hop and musique concrète (Jay Dee, Raymond Scott), between improv and drum'n'bass (Derek Bailey made a recording with some London DnB artists), between Sonic Youth and just about everybody. The smoke of the twentieth century is clearing; the achievements of the past are being properly sought out. New composers, rather than pursuing the "healing" option of '90s new age classical (Gorecki, John Adams, etc.), are instead looking back to the supposedly obsolete, difficult, dodecaphonic European music of the twentieth century, fascinated by the more elaborate challenges it sets. That said, the old guard of the new music, like Pierre Boulez, who yearn for some underlying unity to bind the fragmentation wrought by postmodernism, have probably had their hopes forever dashed.

A similar reinvestigation of the lost utopianism of the twentieth century is currently being undertaken in the art world. One could contrast, as I frequently have done in this text, the fortunes of high art and the relatively cash-starved world of avant-garde music. One could single out Tracey Emin as an example of where conceptual art's idealism has washed up — on the exclusive, sun-kissed shores of elitism. Her works are the property of Tory propagandist Charles Saatchi, her buyers the likes of George Michael, Madonna and The Rolling Stones' Ronnie Wood. There is Rachel Whiteread, whom the pop-group-turned-neo-Dadaist "art terrorist" the K Foundation taunted by setting up an alternative awards ceremony, in which she was voted Worst Artist of the Year. For this, they gave her £40,000, but only when they threatened to burn the prize money did she scurry down and accept it. The K Foundation's work, including their setting fire to a million pounds in cash, mocks what they regard as the self-serving, cash-chasing vacuity of modern art, with Whiteread a hapless participant in one of their most effective stunts.

However, as Dan Fox of *Frieze* points out, such figures, though much publicised, are un-representive of modern art as a whole. "I can assure you, there are still plenty of garrets," he says. "This always needs to be pointed out as a counter against stories of silly money being made. There are hundreds of curators, artists, struggling to make ends meet — as well as writers — who simply believe in what they do, investigate the role that the visual can have in society. People like Damien Hirst, as far as I'm concerned, are no longer interesting. His work, nowadays, borders on kitsch. He's no longer part of any critical dialogue."

Furthermore, even in the high-profile world of conceptual art there is much to celebrate. Take Christo and Jeanne-Claude's wrapping of the Reichstag in 1995, the culmination of several installations in which he bound public structures in fabric. His early efforts look slightly botched by comparison, but by 1995 he had the practicalities of wrapping a large building down to a fine technique. I went to Berlin to see the results. The event was misreported in the UK press as a public flop. It was anything but — throughout its sunny duration, crowds turned out en masse to spectate the Reichstag, resplendent in its cloak of thick, metallic pleats and drapery, its colour changing at various points of the day. It was art, but it was ephemeral — I recall the sense of real sadness, like the inevitable end of a holiday romance when I departed Berlin, knowing that, unlike the great architecture, natural wonders or art treasures of the world, I would never be able to see this again. It was art, but not only was it widely available for all to see, it placed no strain on the public purse of any kind — Christo and Jeanne-Claude raised the money themselves. Christo has claimed that his art has no higher meaning — that he simply wishes to make the world, even if temporarily, a more beautiful place. However, in this case, it did have resonance. The Reichstag was a key building in at least three of the major upheavals of the twentieth century — the First World War, the rise of the Nazis (assisted by the burning of the Reichstag) and the collapse of the Berlin Wall. The wrapped Reichstag felt like a present from the past to the future in a newly unified country, the building symbolically cleansed in its watery cascades of silvery fabric.

Or, maybe that's just so much more feverish and speculative crit-speak masquerading as explanation. Maybe the wrapped Reichstag no more needs to be saddled with political significance than does Doris Salcedo's *Shibboleth*. Maybe it's enough that the wrapped Reichstag did temporarily make the world a more beautiful place, but not even that is a necessity. Some modern music actually makes the world an uglier place — disfigures it, rends its serene surfaces, but is no less gripping or compelling for all that. As Simon Reynolds wrote of noise music in *Blissed Out: The Raptures of Rock*, "The subliminal message of most music is that the world is essentially benign, that if there is sadness, or tragedy, this is resolved at the level of some higher harmony. Noise troubles this worldview."

Finally, the necessity of the useless; much of modern music is about that. A piece of electronic music by Bruno Maderna is too invasive to qualify as ambient. A piece of electronica by Autechre is too arrhythmical to be danced to — like mobile sculptures, these pieces demand to be spectated, for their own sake. They serve no function, require no decoding. As Aaron Copland said, we approach music in "kinda of a dumb way". It does not require a sharp mind, exactly, so much as an open one. Ornette Coleman complained of people who felt they had to "get" something from his music, some tangible, understood return on the attention paid. "I often have people come to me and say, 'I like it but I don't understand it.' Many people, apparently, don't trust their reactions to art or music unless there is a verbal explanation for it."

One of the great reasons avant-garde music needs to exist is that it does not need to exist. It defies, momentarily, the glum, onward and upward propulsion of Western society into which the majority of us are whipped or whip ourselves, on a daily basis. It fails, successfully, to be commandeered into the ranks of function. It posits and evokes entirely alternative modes, worlds, possibilities, stepping off the tramlines and running aground on new, virgin territory. It goes nowhere. It repeats. It radiates energy, wastefully, into the air. It leaks out from the grid. Yet none of this is a reason to condemn it as indulgent, or degenerate. It is the threat it notionally poses to civilisation that makes it so supremely civilised. It is its refusal to be co-opted by the forces that drive us on towards eventual death that makes it so affirmative. The musician Jim O' Rourke once released a single called *Therefore I Am*. That is it, in three words. No need, even for the thinking. So embrace. Immerse. The numbers already doing so may represent a tiny fragment of the overall demographic, but they still run into the millions, all of them in the grip of a collective sanity. As AMM said, What is there in uselessness to cause you distress?

AFTERWORD: 2023

When *Fear of Music* was first published in 2009, the Labour government had been in power for 11 years, Barack Obama president for a matter of months. The political mood, as I felt it at least, was one of torpid disappointment, cynicism, even — a certain lassitude. The right-wing and far-right forces which hold such frightening sway in 2023 felt down and out, an ineffectual laughing stock, on the verge of extinction, perhaps. But the "only-get-better" idealism of 1997 had long dissipated. The early 2000s as a whole had felt like a comedown after the euphoria of the untroubled '90s. If the right was down and out, the left, or the prospect of a more just and inclusive world, felt right off the cards. Politics was a matter of pragmatic mediocrity, and that was that. If you were not the victim of it, you could go days without particularly thinking about it.

Facebook was in its infancy, limited in its letter counts. Twitter was barely a year old. The permanent firestorm of coruscation, assertion and counter-assertion, the "culture wars" and moral panic of our own time were but a flicker on the periphery of social media. David Cameron, with his fresh-faced estate-agency plausibility and promise of a detoxified Tory party, was a year away from charming a bored, somnambulant nation into handing him the keys to No.

10, with promises of a "Big Society", compassion towards hoodies, and abolishing an unpopular ID scheme mooted by authoritarian Labour — before setting about inflicting the cruelty of austerity, the squeezing of public services while private profits inflate obscenely.

Avoidable tragedies like Grenfell, the excess deaths suffered through the Tories' callous mismanagement of COVID, the engineering of a ruinous Brexit, the billions of public money squandered or diverted into the hands of cronies are among the more conspicuously egregious crimes against society committed by a gaggle of some of the most heinous, incompetent, mendacious and cruel Tory ministers ever to have governed this country, the names of whom, Boris Johnson apart, were barely known in 2009.

This despotic cruelty has been emulated, exceeded even, across the world — Orbán in Hungary; Erdoğan in Turkey; Putin, still considered a force for stability by those not fully paying attention in 2009; Bolsonaro in Brazil; and, of course, Donald Trump — awful authoritarian leaders with quasi-fascistic bents, who seemed to threaten not just democracy but life on Earth.

Meanwhile, the left in the UK was subject to a very recognisable political schism when Jeremy Corbyn was elected leader of the UK, setting Labour centrists and leftists at bitter loggerheads, waging war on an increasingly febrile Twitter that still burns. While Twitter (now X) remains, despite Elon Musk, a valuable source of in-depth information, citation and insight somewhat woefully lacking in mainstream media, the increasingly compromised BBC News in particular, it has also become an open sewer for thoughts, obnoxious self-made "characters", and far-right, unabashedly racist rhetoric — the sort of thoughts that in pre-Twitter days had to be confined to swirling in the minds of the wretches who harboured such ideas, or scrawled on toilet walls. Now, they could be posted publically, with the same authority of the printed word, as those of a Stephen Fry. Thanks to Twitter, and in the face of great and articulate antipathy, the far right have gained a foothold in the discourse.

All this, plus the gaslighting and "culture wars" engaged in by an increasingly unhinged right-wing press perhaps conscious of its own impending mortality, has prompted a counterinsurgency, whose stress is on "kindness" in the most radical, active sense of the word — from mental health and neurodivergency to trans rights, anti-racism, and direct action on climate change to an intersectional approach to fighting for the right to be included, even simply, in the face of a grotesque anti-trans moral panic, the right to exist.

While many were hyper-vigilant during the years of lassitude, and many now can quite tranquilly zone out the blare of 2020s' adversarial discourse, it does feel that those working in the arts cannot easily remain in hermetic isolation, solely concerned with aesthetic matters, spatial relationships, and so forth. Social and political contexts are harder to avoid. We really are living in the world, a world afire metaphorically and literally. At the conclusion of this book I discussed, as per AMM, the value of "uselessness", and that still stands. However, whether it be fighting for resources, addressing inclusivity in a cross-the-board, intersectional manner, or directly addressing the current affairs that impact all our lives, the avant garde has a duty to find ways of being useful.

This is certainly happening among avant-garde visual artists. Take Steve McQueen, whose film work has increasingly gravitated towards impassioned takes on race, from his TV series, *Small Axe*, affording a glimpse into the lives of British-based West Indians hitherto not properly chronicled on the small screen. In 2023, there was also his short film *Grenfell*, taken in a single shot from a helicopter, which silently invites the viewer's horror as it contemplates the blackened tower, a living mausoleum as well as a char, a blemish on London, and the British state's ongoing indifference to the health and safety of black British and working-class lives, here sacrificed for the sake of profiteering, corner-cutting property developers.

The Tate, meanwhile, though still not open to sound art, has, in a series of exhibitions, laid stress on women artists — Tacita Dean, Tania Bruguera, Kara Walker, Anicka Yi, Cecilia Vicuña among them — under the directorship of Francis Morris, from 2016 to

2023 in particular, consciously making up for decades of sexist complacency, in which it was supposed that — the odd, outlying tomboy apart — women simply did not apply themselves to the visual arts.

The Tate Modern may not have embraced sound art, but it remains a holdout in this respect. Elsewhere, the silence of galleries has been broken. Shortly after the publication of this book, I was made aware of a project at the National Gallery in which musicians/soundscapers such as Chris Watson, Jem Finer and Simon Fisher Turner were invited to create their own "audio gallery tours" in response to the paintings in the museum collection. Meanwhile, Tate Britain began to host Late at Tate, a series of events in which contemporary musicians have been invited to perform in the setting of the museum's collection of pre-twentieth-century art. These included Tim Whitehead, a jazz musician creating music inspired by and in dialogue with the JMW Turner artwork at the Tate, and a curated event in which eighteenth-century ideas of the sublime were explored through the medium of horns, sub-bass drones, and a performance by three amplified cellists of a piece by Uzbek composer Aziza Sadikova. David Toop, meanwhile, performed at the Tate Britain with his Laptop Orchestra. He noted that performing in a gallery "governed the behaviour" of those who came to see him perform. Some of the attentive reverence with which they were accustomed to viewing avant-garde art rubbed off as they witnessed an avant-garde music spectacle in the gallery.

As curator Madeleine Keep explained to me at the time, there was a practical reason why Tate Britain were putting on such events. Unlike the Tate Modern, Tate Britain does not have much "passer-by traffic" and has to think harder about the sorts of events it puts on to attract visitors — be that much more imaginative. It also meant expanding the museum's visiting hours, with events running into mid-evening, alcohol served and live music played, expanding the idea of what it means to visit a gallery. "They have come to be surprised — they come in a very open frame of mind," he said. Still, he did recall a couple of ladies who demurred, "men with laptops — disgusting," a rather less open frame of mind which held that these so-called "artists" were probably staring at porn on their screens.

Gabriel Prokofiev, grandson of the famous Sergei, puts on a variety of events under the aegis of his Nonclassical banner, in which he brings contemporary classical music into unlikely juxtapositions — in pub settings, or subject to techno remixes. He played a recent event at the Tate featuring a performance of his *Concerto for Turntables and Orchestra No. 1* by DJ Switch. Again, although being a gallery was distracting, people felt free to move about from room to room. Prokofiev found that the gallery's context boosted the respectfulness of those in attendance.

It is hard, then and now, to dispel an air of self-consciousness about these undertakings, to reconcile these worlds apart. Turntablist, composer, and performer Mariam Rezaei has performed in galleries and wryly notes the "extra zero" on the end of her performance fee as opposed to the upstairs rooms at pubs and similar spaces, in which improv musicians and their audiences generally muster. She has worked, too, to bridge the gap between turntablism and orchestral music, in her quest to have the turntable recognised not just as a token of hip-hop but also as a legitimate instrument in its own right, as well as querying the very nature of "composition". "People underestimate the turntable, and as someone who gets it, I realise how much potential there is for the new, the unheard, and the unimagined. To me, that's the raison d'être for musicians. I can see the potential of the turntable. I can see its potential for the next 200 years. I can hear it."

Mariam Rezaei was brought up in economically depressed working-class Gateshead, in the North East of England. Her father being Iranian, she was one of just two people of colour at her school, the other being her twin brother. Today, she has a number of acclaimed projects to her name, including her 2022 piece *SADTITZZZ*, a "requiem for turntablism", a three-way live turntable project with Maria Chávez and Victoria Shen, as well as having shared the bill with Art Ensemble of Chicago's Roscoe

Mitchell at a titanic gig at London's Iklectik. She is one of a number of British-Iranian musicians working at the vanguard of sonic experimentalism, one of a far greater number of women of colour worldwide working in this field. Talking to her via Zoom, however, is a chastening, inspiring story, not just of what it is like to come upon this music from absolutely nowhere but also of the obstacles and hindrances she has had to face along the way — discouragement, condescension, inadequate resources, lack of funding, misapprehension, a culture of machismo in her chosen field. "I feel like I've fought fucking hard for a long time," she sighs.

Already fired by an ambition to play at the Royal Albert Hall at age five, her first instrument was a £50 piano bought from a charity shop, her first lessons given by a "little old lady". Her ambitions were constantly knocked back — *Why not just sing Disney songs like any other musically bright little girl?* — but at least she got to practise piano instead of going to school assembly in the morning.

In her teens, she found herself going to parties, steeped in techno and hip-hop. She was intrigued by the DJ's role and the control they had of the party. Her epiphany came when seeing the German DJ David, sometime DMC World Champion, which opened up to her the possibilities of turntable manipulation as a music form and of the turntable as an instrument in its own right. She found that her advanced skills and dexterity as a keyboard player were quite portable to the art of turntablism.

She attempted to involve herself in the battling culture of turntablism, in which you had to prove yourself, like DJ David, through feats of speed and virtuosity. However, she would soon tire of the attritional macho tendency of battling and competing, the sexist expectations of her as a woman, as well as the limited set of criteria that determined "success" in battle. Studying for music A-level with the local council (her school could only teach her to GCSE level), she met other composers who opened up to her the world of contemporary music, from Shostakovich to Fluxus, abstract music, graphic scores — she had an inkling of a freedom possible in music, as well as a musical culture that was about collaboration, camaraderie, mutual support, and the unfettered exploration of ideas.

That said, Rezaei by no means forsook the hip-hop aspect of her introduction to turntablism in favour of the "higher", groundbreaking, conceptual work of the likes of John Cage. "It's really important that we start breaking down the hierarchy. We need to stop tokenising the turntable. It's important we talk about John Cage, Schaeffer, Daphne Oram, Christian Marclay, but they're not the only ones, and there's so much that is undiscovered. Also, for me, it's not so much about who does it first as who does it best. Hip-hop does not get enough of the credit for what it's done. It didn't invent turntablism, but it made it bloom and blossom into something so magnificent."

One artist who did inspire her was the German composer Paul Hindemith. On 18 June 1930, at a concert of modern music in Berlin that evening were three *Originalwerke für Schallplatten* by Hindemith and Ernst Toch. The duo would record music onto discs, then further manipulate them by altering the speed and direction of the discs during playback. No performers were involved; it was a means, in pre-electronic times, of exploring new timbral and textural possibilities through the newfound art of manipulation. The practice, briefly popular, soon fell into disuse, but for Rezaei, "it feels like my work has more to do with what they did then, what's being going on for the best part of 90 years — that they wrote music to put onto records to further manipulate as a process — has a curiosity to it, an element of freeness that a lot of other turntablism don't".

Rezaei's projects represent an exploratory quest for freedom, as represented in the limitless possibilities of the turntable as instrument — non-linear, rotational, able to mess with time itself, able to make anything from anything. Her work is at once beautifully, disconcertingly abstract, using repetition yet vast in its range, aleatoric, embracing chance as a factor in the shape and direction of her pieces but at the same time drawing on her virtuosity as a turntablist, in which she retains a battler's fierce pride. She speaks of reviews that appear to question whether she achieves the sound weave she does on turntables alone. "There's no Ableton — that's pure sweat and blood!"

Crucially, Rezaei is not remote or hermetic in her practice. Much of her current work is made in explicit solidarity with women in Iran, courageously defying the violent, patriarchal theocracy of that country. As someone active on the arts scene in the North East, she wants better access in the arts for non-binary, trans people, people of colour, people with access needs. "The solution is multi-pronged — I don't want to sit and profess what the future should be; I just want to make it happen."

Rezaei's story is just one of many across the UK, across the world. Many such battles are being fought on many fronts. Hers is exemplary.

In 1968, the album *Switched-On Bach*, credited to the American composer Walter Carlos, was released. It comprised versions of pieces by Johann Sebastian Bach, rendered on the Moog synthesiser. It was a painstaking and protracted process, with pieces having to be recorded one note at a time on the monophonic synthesiser, which was also apt to drift out of tune. The album, however, was a huge success. While one can sympathise with Pierre Boulez, who dismissed it as "gimmicky" in its somewhat literal transcriptions, it served very well as a demonstration of the capabilities of the Moog synth, and, in that respect, was groundbreaking. Carlos would go on to work with directors such as Stanley Kubrick and has remained a household name.

It was only in 1979 that Carlos revealed that she had undergone gender reassignment surgery several years earlier and now went by the name Wendy. *Switched-On Bach* had placed her under huge personal pressure because she was already well down the road of her gender confirmation process — she had been conscious of this when a child. In the late '60s, however, having attained a surprising level of fame, she felt forced to disguise herself as "Walter", her dead name, and conceal her transitioning status. According to her biographer, Amanda Sewell, when making public appearances, she would adopt a deeper voice, use makeup to give her face an unshaven effect, and wear a wig and pasted-on sideburns.

When she finally did reveal her true identity, she said, "the public turned out to be amazingly tolerant or, if you wish, indifferent [...] There had never been any need of this charade to have taken place. It had proven a monstrous waste of years of my life."

Different times, perhaps. Since then, she has remained reclusive but with no great interest in advocating for the trans community, despite being the most high-profile trans person in music. "She was a 'normal' woman, and that was the end of it," wrote Sewell. Nor did she seek to correlate her work with her status as a trans woman.

Are there such correlations? One wonders if the non-binary, gender fluidity has an altering effect on the sensibility of trans practitioners. Take Terre Thaemlitz, for example, aka DJ Sprinkles, a musician who has exercised a huge influence trans people working in the avant/experimental regions of dance and ambient. Thaemlitz's work, which also stretches into academia, ranges and shapeshifts from dancefloor, to minimal ambient, mutations of pop, including Gary Numan's *Cars*, as well as heavily sampled pieces which directly address issues around transitioning, upturn conventional expectations. In a 2013 lecture delivered at the Tate, Thaemlitz said: "As someone fitting into an MTF (male to female) category, hereby I am instantly expected to be campy, upbeat and entertaining, I have gone to great lengths in my own performances to present an alternative transgendered stage that forgoes both glamour and trash in favour of critical minded boredom and uneventfulness."

Other artists, such as Lorelei Kretsinger of the Missouri-based queer and trans music collective Un/Tuck, believes that being trans significantly impacts her practice as an electronic musician. "I'm not speaking for every trans person, but for me, it can be a lot more nerve-racking to go outside and perform," she told the *Guardian*'s Jude Rogers in 2020. "So I spend time at home honing my production skills. It's also liberating to be able to express yourself online, to create your own world."

Or there is the late SOPHIE, Scottish DJ and producer, whose 2018 hyperpop *Oil of Every Pearl's Un-Insides* is a masterpiece of "becoming", pitch shifting, Auto-Tune in full effect, morphing from candy-coated pop to barrages of ear-grinding noise, ranges fluidly from honeyed R&B melodies to brutal abstraction.

Brighton-based Catherine Backhouse, aka Xylitol, who makes music in remote realms where IDM leaves off, ghostly traces of post-DnB that feel far away from Earth, tells her story. It's one of many. This is hers.

I suppose my coming-to-awareness of my trans-ness has been quite intimately connected to my engagement with music. In the '90s and 2000s dancing, whether at techno clubs or more overtly queer spaces like Kash Point gave me a space to explore my sense of being a body in the world in ways that weren't open to me in my everyday life. There was a shedding of gendered expectations on the dancefloor which in a way seemed to open up a sense of alternate possibility even if it would take a decade or two for me to come to any tangible realisation of what that could mean and how I could inhabit this. The vocabulary of queerness I guess felt like a rarefied terrain at that time. I knew queer people and went to queer spaces and felt welcome there, but also had a reflexive denial of my own place within it. Like a tourist. In terms of my own music, I think at that time the tension is there within it: a desire for female subjecthood and a reflexive need to deny it. There's an uncomfortable terseness about it and a fear of the sensual.

> I venerated Felix Kubin, Chicks On Speed, Peaches as well as the sound experiments, dance tracks and, maybe just as importantly, interviews and essays by Terre Thaemlitz/DJ Sprinkles. I felt Thaemlitz spoke my language regarding gender, music and capitalism and opened up a space within the queer discourse — for want of a better term — that I felt comfortable in. A kind of a portal. Before I transitioned, I was attempting to sublimate the desire I felt to divest myself

> of gender (or — in retrospect — the expectations my assigned gender placed upon me) through music — as a means to escape myself and inhabit another body, to dissolve my fractured sense of identity into something kind of amorphous; but it felt the more I attempted to do this, the more violently what I would later understand as gender dysphoria would fracture and undo this momentary illusion of wholeness.
>
> While my approaches to making music haven't changed significantly over the decade of my medical and social transition, I feel much more able to explore sounds, melodies, loops, rhythms and sequences without feeling a need to undercut, deconstruct or self-critique. I want to explore what my music can do for bodies immersed in it, just as dancing to techno, jungle and krautrock gave me, if only for a fleeting ecstatic moment on the dancefloor, the psychic space to re-imagine what my body could do and what it could become. I'm absolutely inspired by the trans and queer artists that have emerged in the wake of SOPHIE — I adore felicita, Hyd, Elysia Crampton, DJ Girl; the gleeful trash pop of 100 gecs and the melancholia of Black Dresses, etc., etc. I'm not sure how my music fits in with those artists, although I'm keen to explore making pop music again. But just suffice to say the nightclub remains a vital space in which divergent genders are imagined and nurtured and is the space that I want to continue to inhabit.

The improv scene remains a tiny haven for thousands upon thousands of tiny flames across the world. It persists on a pittance. Although it has long outlived the disparaging attitudes of such established composers as Luciano Berio that improv musicians were but a feral species compared with the grand architects of classical composition. However, its informality means that improv must be practised in the tiniest of spaces, shut out from the sort of structures and institutions which provide the sort of funding that enables musicians to focus entirely on their music making.

Still, this at least affords what David Toop refers to as the "dream of freedom", which improv represents, in which the only protocol to be observed is the principle of listening. I must confess that in 2009, I harboured the fear that improv's main practitioners would be the last generation to bear the mantle of the genre; one particularly senior line-up at an event around the time made me wonder if the music were the equivalent of the Cornish tin mines, prone to extinction.

Happily, not only are most of that generation not only surviving but still playing, still probing, but they are being followed up by waves of younger practitioners too, blowing, scraping, bowing and tweaking across the full gamut of instruments — percussion, brass, strings, accordions, guitars, keyboards, vocals, loop pedals, laptops, analogue electronics, found objects.

In recent years, the gigs in which I have taken by far the most pleasure have not been stadium affairs, mega-singalongs to the still popular, still active pop and rock stars of yesteryear, partying like it's 1999, 1989, 1979, 1969, nor in mid-size venues where there is nowadays a tense expectation that some idiot or idiots are going to talk over the music. They have been in upstairs rooms, café basements, huts, crucial, low capacity venues like the Iklektik in Waterloo or the 100 Years gallery in East London, events like Linear Obsessional or Scaledown. These are intimate events, sometimes housing as few as 12 or 15 people, with funding consisting of a tin passed round or CD sales. They can be strikingly good-humoured, social events for regulars and music appreciators, but once the music strikes up, everyone falls silent, everyone listens, including, of course, the musicians to each other: the deep, exploratory conversations without language of which improv so often consists, as if working in a collective trance to achieve spontaneous creation. Sets are usually short to accommodate a greater number of musicians — and the standard of playing is extremely high, the mark met by more musicians than the market can bear, in reality. But there is no battling, except the battle for self-realisation. The scene is inclusive, intimate, humble, a paradigm of extreme tolerance, extreme democracy, and, for the listener, an uncommonly rewarding experience rather than some sort of austere chore, as outsiders might imagine. And absolutely free. So long as there are instruments, this navigation of the outer reaches of musical curiosity will persist.

One of the strangest examples of first contact between the avant-garde and a mass audience followed the release of the final stage of The Caretaker's (aka Leyland Kirby) *Everywhere at the End of Time*. The Caretaker is an allusion to Jack Nicholson's character in Stanley Kubrick's 1980 film *The Shining*, in which he plays an author looking after a Colorado hotel during its off season. In order to enhance its horrific supernatural effects, Kubrick, as we have seen, resorted to the music of twentieth-century composers such as Bartók and Ligeti, though their music was not composed with the sole intention of "horrifying". Eeriest of all, however, are the reverberant sections of ballroom music, signifying the lingering, ghostlike present of former occupants of the hotel (including Nicholson's author himself, it appears).

This was the element upon which The Caretaker drew in his ongoing, six-and-a-half-hour track, as he subjected his source material — 78 rpm records of ballroom music — to increasing degradation, as if to mimic the processes of mental decay that eventuates in full-on dementia.

It is, indeed, a distressing, if conceptually ingenious piece of music, not least because of its stated purpose, one for which you do need to brace yourself. It opens with *It's Just a Burning Memory*, the pleasant, olde worlde sway of a big band tea dance number, which has you sashaying mentally across some imaginary pre-war dancefloor. As the tracks progress, it is as if they are receding into the fog of time, becoming gradually less distinct, a common enough tactic in TV and film soundtracks to denote wistfulness, bittersweet poignancy. But the deterioration does not end there. By *Stage 5*, in the track *Sudden Time Regression into Isolation*, the source material abides but in cut-up, intermittent form, the linear fragments of what have been now worn down to grainy, white noise forming an inescapable mental labyrinth, the reverberation now generating a thick fog, all of which intensifies the isolation of the title. So it is also with *Synapse Retrogenesis*. If these were just abstracts, then those who find great musical pleasure in noise could enjoy these pieces on a textural basis. It's much harder to do so knowing what this project is about, what it consciously intends: to convey what anguish and confusion is raging in the mind of a person quiet, sedentary, stiff, with late stage dementia.

Somehow, the piece became a sort of "dare" on TikTok — users of the site took it on themselves to see how long they could endure this otherworldly cacophony purporting to be music. Young listeners documented their reactions and The Caretaker hashtag would go on to attain well over seven million views.

What is notable however is that, far from treating The Caretaker's music as a sort of Jackass for the ears, that listeners initiated into it found it moving, disturbing, relatable in an empathetic way. Some reflected on their own, more spiritual sense of alienation and isolation from what they considered a "real" sense of selfhood.

Looking at the many YouTube comments, the following is typical. "This is the last embers of awareness the person has before they become little more than a bedridden corpse, with only darkness, silence and the occasional incoherent fragment of memory to accompany them, until terminal lucidity and death (or in many cases just death). Some of the background noises sound like voices screaming in horror at this prospect, as the patient sinks into the abyss of emptiness."

And this, with *Stage 6* still to come. At the time of writing, the full album of *Stage 6* recordings, in which the sense of desolation and detachment from the source material is still greater, more terrifying, though not without a bleak beauty, continues to enthral rather than repel listeners, alive to its deathly sadness. Among the near 4000 comments on the YouTube site are those who have watched grandparents afflicted by the disease. Others take a sort of comfort in the finality implied by its grey, flat, near-deathly expanses of dark ambience. I'm reminded of my grandmother with her lucid reminiscences of her Edwardian childhood interspersed with moments of failure to recognise others in her encroaching senility — also, that rapt terror I felt when I first heard the *Region IV* of Stockhausen's *Hymnen* as a 15-year-old.

The kids are all right. Moving further "infield", into the post-rock, post-pop landscape, in which there is no longer the sort of weekly continuum, the sense of an ever-shifting narrative driven by now extinct institutions like *Smash Hits*, *Top of the Pops* and the weekly music press, it's harder to get a foothold on what happening. No one knows what is Number One any more, and despite the monstrous share of the pie they enjoy, it is, I've found, quite possible to move through the world without knowingly hearing any track at all by Ed Sheeran, Taylor Swift or Adele.

My daughter Alisha, just turned 18, has been urging her music on me in recent years, though without taking any reciprocal interest in any of my suggestions to her. I note among the assorted hip-hop and emo-tinged pieces she sends me a sense of mid-tempo enervation, of moroseness manifested in both the often spoken word vocals, of layered production words which add to the sense of sweet drag. It's as if this music speaks to a generation more melancholic, more sober, more conscious of the weight of the world to come than their forebears were at the same age.

For her sake, I decided to take a deeper Spotify dive into artists to whom I've failed to pay proper attention over these past few years — Frank Ocean, Stormzy, Beyoncé Knowles and her sister Solange. One factor I found in common with them was a certain, dark limpidity, as if they had drawn from the wells of Stevie Wonder's Moog-soaked balladry of the early '70s — again, that sense that the euphoria that obtained in the 1990s was a speck on a receding horizon.

I was struck also at how avant-garde their productions were, certainly by comparison with previous generations. The weave of beats, samples, layers felt daringly original, irregular, intricate, cliché and trope avoidant, if not exactly dissonant. Beyoncé is a particularly interesting case in point. While I found her 2022 *Renaissance* a bit over-rich, over-determined to pack every last pixel with some sort of idea, or top-of-the-range musical feature, its predecessor, *Lemonade* feels like her masterpiece, a pinnacle of 21st century pop.

What strikes me is that Beyoncé is such a commercially formidable artist. It is as if she is a corporation in her own right, a touring, self-advertising, self-asserting, money-making piece of machinery, depressingly prone to making money by playing some unsavoury gigs, including $24m for a private concert in Dubai, which made her supposed "progressive" values seem like so much soulwashing.

And yet, the productions on *Lemonade*, a determinedly commercial album, are progressive indeed, in no way compromised, or lowest common denominator. It can feel that *Lemonade*'s drive for originality and excellence is akin to that of a luxury brand, for which it is imperative not to sink to the level of downmarket tat, but certainly, among her collaborators it is clear that audacity of musical thought is actively encouraged and harvested, rather than rejected.

Hold Up is a case in point. It's a work of minimal genius, so much so that's its hard to imagine what its co-creators — Diplo, Ezra Koenig, Beyoncé, Emile Haynie, Josh Tillman, MNEK and MeLo-X — all found to contribute to its 3′41″ duration; and, if you factor in Doc Pomus and Mort Shuman, composers of Andy Williams's *Can't Get Used To Losing You*, which the song samples to inspired effect, or Brian Chase, Karen O and Nick Zinner, who wrote The Yeah Yeah Yeah's *Maps*, an interpolation of which features here, likewise *Turn My Swag On*, written by Soulja Boy, Antonio Randolph and Kevin McConnell, still harder.

And yet, the song works, not just as a pop song but in its juxtapositions, details, layering and invisible craft, as a piece of left-field music the like of which you might expect from a Holly Herndon or Maria Minerva. Yes, you could argue that this is creation by committee, and that's certainly something I feel overwhelmingly on *Renaissance*, but here, one is struck by the ingenuity simply of assembling such an array of contributors, all encouraged to come up with their very best, rather than merely expedient, ear-catching, serviceable ideas. Clearly, contemporary technologies allow for a much richer sonic experience, micro-detail, application of overmatter that has helped transport the likes of Beyoncé to the level of an avant-garde pop aristocracy. What's certain is we are a long, long way from the dull, formulaic thud of Stock, Aitken & Waterman.

As for (post-) rock, yes, it reached a quandary, a terminus back in the early 1990s when it could no longer expand and develop sonically, as it had from the 1960s onwards, without spilling into the realms on the non-commercial, the abstract. Commercially successful rock music, unlike pop, would have to be confined to the retrograde hereafter.

It's heartening, however, in 2023, to see three old avant-garde stalwarts not only maintaining their form, despite their members being in most cases well into their sixties, still evolving, producing some of the best music of their lives, not least because of the accumulation of their experience. So, Swans, led by Michael Gira, with *Beggar* created a monumentalist, epic sound, an advance on anything they had produced heretofore, not least as a result of the history and understanding Gira had developed with longtime co-musicians and a cumulative battery of instrumentation incorporated over the years. Pere Ubu, meanwhile, whose 2019 album *The Long Goodbye* had been intended as valedictory, owing to lead singer David Thomas's health issues, came roaring back on all cylinders in 2023 with *Trouble on Big Beat Street*, a rejuvenated Thomas embarking on fresh narrative landscapes, coloured in and shaped by longtime collaborators with decades of mutual understanding between them. Finally, Creep Show, featuring the brilliant John Grant and also Stephen Mallinder, active since co-founding Cabaret Voltaire in 1972, released their second album, *Yawning Abyss*, on which Grant and Mallinder produce a series of extreme vocal manipulations and vocoderisations of dazzling variation and virtuosity which, using existing technologies in an unprecedentedly imaginative way, laying down a new marker for what can be done with the voice in popular music, exploding pre-existing notions with cubistic radicalism. Veterans creating futures I, for one, had dared not, could not imagine.

In 2019, Merle Hazard, a country singer who specialises in tuneful ditties touching on topics such as hyperinflation in the Weimar Republic and the prospects for the US economy during a period of low interest rates, put out on YouTube his latest number, *(Gimme Some of That) Ol' Atonal Music*. To an accompaniment featuring stand-up bass, fiddle and a top-notch atonal banjo solo, Hazard reminisces regretfully about his late father, a composer of serial music; "Now, Papa's compositions came in rigid 12-tone rows/There was no tonal center to the music he composed", trills Hazard, in decidedly tonal, Nashville-style verse. However, he laments, "Since dear 'ol Daddy left us, life has been so hard/There aren't enough musicians who embrace the avant-garde." This is a terrible shame, sings Hazard; "emotion is for simple folk/art should be arcane".

Hazard's magnificent labour of love for both country and modern classical does raise a pertinent question. What is the status of the pioneers of the music so fervently embraced by his dear old Pops? Schoenberg, Webern, Alban Berg? Of the three, the relatively lush Berg is the most likely to receive a concert hall airing in 2023, while Webern, minimal to the point of evanescence has an abiding allure, but it's hard to disagree with author Stephen Walsh, who, in a 2018 volume about Debussy, wrote that "Schoenberg may be the first 'great' composer in modern history whose music has not entered the repertoire almost a century and a half after his birth." This is borne out also by musician friends of mine such as Julia McDonnell, who recalls a great emphasis on Schoenberg at her university training in Australia but, since coming to the UK, rarely being asked to perform his works at all.

The question is, is there a great onus, an imperative to listen to Schoenberg in 2023? Why should musicians, listeners adhere to the diktats of serialism, decried to me by Can's Irmin Schmidt, classically trained and a one time Kapellmeister as "Stalinist"? Moreover, as the composer and podcaster Samuel Andreyev has pointed out, Schoenberg was "simultaneously a conservative and a radical", whose innovations were not intended to explode the tradition of Central European classical music, but to renew and preserve it. The progress of avant-garde music has been away from the hegemonic European centre occupied by the great architect of modernity, away from his dogma, away from his dead, white maleness, across the world, across other cultures.

None of this is good enough reason to dispense with Schoenberg. Firstly, the reason his music does not get a wider airing is not out of a desire to get away from the European hegemony in mainstream concert programmers, but much more likely out of a simple, ongoing conservatism. Secondly, despite the aura of difficulty that still fogs Schoenberg, his music is really not anything like so gruelling or austere, or rigid in form for that matter, as Mr Hazard teasingly suggests. As Andreyev observes, in its zealous avoidance of repetition, its mercurial desire to exist only in the moment, its unpredictability, its blazing, expressionist colour, all ensure that any sense of "challenge" quickly fades away, especially on repeated exposure. As my friend Mark Pringle — whose musical journey has taken him from near-chart success with the Heather Smalls-fronted soul band Hot House in the '80s to his current improv project (with Adam Brett and Laura Hills), A Beast with Three Backs — put it, "I've become quite fond of 12-tone, without remotely understanding the theory behind it. And that may be a way into it, by ignoring all that dogma and simply listening to it."

Jazz writer Stewart Smith, meanwhile, a chronicler of the great modern jazz revival of the twenty-first century in the face of the conservatism represented by the likes of Wynton Marsalis, which is a story in itself, says, "It's still something people play with but in a less rigid way," and advises checking out Ingrid Laubrock's *The Last Quiet Place* "for some spicy tone row action. Broadly speaking,

I think the focus in new music just now is on timbre and tuning." He isn't wrong.

In its diffuseness, twenty-first-century art mirrors the music scene as a whole. The absence of any dominant scene, from, say, a Dada for the twenty-first century (though the vast majority of people had no idea such a thing was occurring just over a century ago) or some Britpop-style art movement to excite media commentators in the febrile, self-regarding United Kingdom, can make it feel like nothing is happening. In fact, everything is happening, everywhere, all at once.

Nevertheless, this lack of any sense of a Great Leap Forward does leave a sense of historical stasis; the past looms inescapably, seemingly larger with each passing decade.

The most recent attempt to market what still remains modern art is to render it immersive. Immersive", like "hub" or "icon" is one of those words which has become as shop soiled as it is ubiquitous as the century has worn on. "Immersive" is, as discussed, the condition painted art has had the most difficulty with in matching music. Traditionally it cannot exceed the sightline of the viewer, however large scale or overwhelming. It is merely in front of you, to be beholden and to be departed from as and when the beholder is inclined.

In the 2020s, there has been an increase in efforts to render painted art "immersive", an experience you can walk through, be bombarded by from all sides, front to rear, floor to ceiling. In the case of the artist David Hockney and his 2023 exhibition, *Bigger and Closer*, he is at least alive and able to direct and devise the experience. However, in the case of, for example, Van Gogh, the nineteenth century would have no notion of how an immersive experience might have worked, and we have no notion of how he might have adjusted his artistic intentions had he had the technical wherewithal to do so.

I decided to brace myself and attend the Dalí "immersive" experience at The Boiler House, Brick Lane, London. Brace myself, for my expectations were not boosted by promotional literature which promised "a walk through Dalí's iconic works — quite literally". The Dalí estate had, however, in the spirit of Avida Dollars, given their approval to the exhibition, which has been a great success.

There is a strong and indeed fair suggestion in the introductory notes at the exhibition that Dalí had a great interest in cybernetics, the "fourth dimension" and would undoubtedly have thrilled to the prospect of seeing his work displayed as it is here, a prospect just out of reach in his own lifetime. No doubt the spectacle of the atomic particles being being beamed stealing and swarming across the exhibition floor would have had the ends of his moustaches twirling with electric delectation; "the jumping and the rumping" as he once enthused in pure Dalínese to Malcolm Muggeridge in a TV interview.

In the main hall, all the familiar Dalían tropes — soft watches, broken eggs, skinny-legged elephants, his wife and muse Gala, passive and queenly — are presented in a Sensurround format, with patrons looking on from the vantage point of beanbags or deckchairs. The blurb promises you that what are you experiencing is akin to being inside the brain of Dalí — a cerebral immersion if you will — but this is as daft a claim as asserting that being in a hall swirling with images of Yorick's skull, Ophelia's drowned corpse, King Henries and Bottom the weaver would be an accurate replication of the mind of Shakespeare. "He is interested in everything and wants to know anything", the curators say of Dalí, and such a psychological, neurological impulsive condition, inflamed by genius, unbound by conventional constrictions and, some would say, scruples, God alone could possibly convey.

The images whoosh around the room, though even then, the limits of the experience do come a cropper as your eye is drawn towards the rafters, the functional piping and girders of the building's ceiling, the edge of the "frame", so to speak. There's an AI section — Dalían images generated automatically, without human intervention, which is is mildly notable, though also a reminder that as things stand, all AI is ultimately entirely dependent on human input.

The dismay I feel at this exhibition is similar to that I felt when the VAR (video assistant referee) technology was introduced into football. It felt needlessly invasive and raised the question, had the game not coped perfectly well, enthralled sufficiently, without this new technology? Similarly with Dalí, has he not been more than fully and adequately appreciated over the past 100 years? The "immersive" experience feels like a piece of elaborate kit designed, in part, to do your imagining for you.

The exhibition concludes with a virtual reality room, with the viewer invited to take headsets and step on deck for a "voyage" across the sands of Dalí's animal and mineral world, with Gala, as ever, looming large — eggs explode, lobsters scuttle. I'd actually recommend the entire exhibition for this alone, not because it represents some critical aesthetic breakthrough but because, well, as my fellow art critics, a group of teenage schoolkids opined, "Wooah!" I have nothing more profound to say to that. I'd recommend it the way I might recommend a fireworks display, as well as the scarcity of the VR headset experience, which remains far from commonplace in twenty-first-century lives and has retained its novelty.

What ultimately galls about the exhibition, and which sadly affirms the ongoing avant-garde music/art divide, is that the exhibition is soundtracked, as if to concede that true "immersion" cannot be achieved without a sonic dimension. There are countless contemporary musicians working in electronics, collage, liberated by laptop technologies, who could have created a workable equivalent to the sensation, surprise, the consternation provoked by Dalí's paintings. The late Holger Czukay of Can, music's closets relation to Dalí, whose solo work, with its own recurring motifs flurries of elephantine horns, samples of John Paul II and distinctive guitar tunings rearing large in the mix, would theoretically have been a fine choice had his life and creative powers been prolonged.

As it is, however, the exhibition's soundtrack dares venture into territory no more radical than some familiar neoclassical sprinkles of Erik Satie and some tonal, melancholic wisps of jazz in the exhibition's introductory room. In the main hall, a thunderous blandness prevails — ponderous, portentous sweeps of instrumentation, dilute trip-hop, synth tones scampering over studiously familiar rhythmical cadences, punctuated banally by, for example, the sound of trumpeting elephants. This is music that, while taking itself rather seriously, as befits its location in a gallery, is designed to placate, not to provoke. It was doubtlessly commissioned with that particular remit in mind. The exhibition's curators would have known full well that while Dalí has an inbuilt decades-old cachet among habitual Tate Modern goers attracted also by the novelty of "immersiveness", a great many of them would have been driven to distress by prolonged exposure to any music that adventured beyond the sort of predictably dramatic language you might expect from a BBC One natural history programme, in which the elephants have sensibly sized legs and the lobsters are the size you'd expect. Uneasy viewing, easy listening. And so, in this respect at least, the premise of this book is sadly still borne out in 2023.

It need not be. In 2023, the German free jazz saxophonist Peter Brötzmann died. The next edition of Stewart Smith's *Jazz Police* was dedicated to Brötzmann's music. Brötzmann had long been on my "to do" list. For whatever reason, I'd never got around to investigating his work properly.

As I switched on, it hit me. This was all the effort that was required, to switch on, to tune in. As the torrents of Brötzmann's raging, joyful sax blew over me, I was reminded once again — but this time with a particular, blazing lucidity — this isn't difficult. This is easy. This is easy listening, a painless but purgative enema for the brain, cascading, avoiding clichés with a raw and supreme determination. It's easy, this twisting, detoxifying, honking, spewing, natural force, clean, filthy, summoned from the gut, the lungs, the lifeblood of a master.

It's easy, this infinite energy, infinite affirmative, energy, this furious peace, this endless, propulsive invention, unfurling upward into the avant yet channelling the spirit, the very bellows of foundational New Orleans jazz, flowing like underground lava across America, across the Atlantic, Pacific. Protest music, as serious as your life, liberation music, as political as your life, from Buddy Bolden to Charlie Haden and all points beyond.

Easy. Nothing to fear. It's happened, it's happening, it will happen, so let it happen to you.

CULTURE, SOCIETY & POLITICS

Contemporary culture has eliminated the concept and public figure of the intellectual. A cretinous anti-intellectualism presides, cheer-led by hacks in the pay of multinational corporations who reassure their bored readers that there is no need to rouse themselves from their stupor. Zer0 Books knows that another kind of discourse — intellectual without being academic, popular without being populist — is not only possible but already flourishing. Zer0 is convinced that in the unthinking, blandly consensual culture in which we live, critical and engaged theoretical reflection is more important than ever before.

Bestsellers from Zer0 Books include:

Poor but Sexy
Culture Clashes in Europe East and West
Agata Pyzik
How the East stayed East and the West stayed West.
Paperback:978-1-78099-394-2 ebook: 978-1-78099-395-9

An Anthropology of Nothing in Particular
Martin Demant Frederiksen
A journey into the social lives of meaninglessness.
Paperback: 978-1-78535-699-5 ebook: 978-1-78535-700-8

In the Dust of This Planet
Horror of Philosophy vol. 1
Eugene Thacker
In the first of a series of three books on the Horror of Philosophy, *In the Dust of This Planet* offers the genre of horror as a way of thinking about the unthinkable.
Paperback: 978-1-84694-676-9 ebook: 978-1-78099-010-1

The End of Oulipo?
An Attempt to Exhaust a Movement
Lauren Elkin, Veronica Esposito
Paperback: 978-1-78099-655-4 ebook: 978-1-78099-656-1

Capitalist Realism
Is There No Alternative?
Mark Fisher
An analysis of the ways in which capitalism has presented itself as the only realistic political-economic system.
Paperback: 978-1-84694-317-1 ebook: 978-1-78099-734-6

Rebel Rebel
Chris O'Leary
David Bowie: every single song. Everything you want to know, everything you didn't know.
Paperback: 978-1-78099-244-0 ebook: 978-1-78099-713-1

Cartographies of the Absolute
Alberto Toscano, Jeff Kinkle
An aesthetics of the economy for the twenty-fi rst century.
Paperback: 978-1-78099-275-4 ebook: 978-1-78279-973-3

Malign Velocities
Accelerationism and Capitalism
Benjamin Noys
Long listed for the Bread and Roses Prize 2015, *Malign Velocities* argues against the need for speed, tracking acceleration as the symptom of the ongoing crises of capitalism.
Paperback: 978-1-78279-300-7 ebook: 978-1-78279-299-4

Babbling Corpse
Vaporwave and the Commodifi cation of Ghosts
Grafton Tanner
Paperback: 978-1-78279-759-3 ebook: 978-1-78279-760-9

New Work New Culture
Work we want and a culture that strengthens us
Frithjof Bergmann
A serious alternative for humankind and the planet.
Paperback: 978-1-78904-064-7 ebook: 978-1-78904-065-4

Romeo and Juliet in Palestine
Teaching Under Occupation
Tom Sperlinger
Life in the West Bank, the nature of pedagogy and the role of a university under occupation.
Paperback: 978-1-78279-637-4 ebook: 978-1-78279-636-7

Color, Facture, Art and Design
Iona Singh
This materialist definition of fine art develops guidelines for architecture, design, cultural studies, and ultimately, social change.
Paperback: 978-1-78099-629-5 ebook: 978-1-78099-630-1

Sweetening the Pill
or How We Got Hooked on Hormonal Birth Control
Holly Grigg-Spall
Has contraception liberated or oppressed women?
Sweetening the Pill breaks the silence on the dark side of hormonal contraception.
Paperback: 978-1-78099-607-3 ebook: 978-1-78099-608-0

Why Are We the Good Guys?
Reclaiming Your Mind from the Delusions of Propaganda
David Cromwell
A provocative challenge to the standard ideology that Western power is a benevolent force in the world.
Paperback: 978-1-78099-365-2 ebook: 978-1-78099-366-9

The Writing on the Wall
On the Decomposition of Capitalism and its Critics
Anselm Jappe, Alastair Hemmens
A new approach to the meaning of social emancipation.
Paperback: 978-1-78535-581-3 ebook: 978-1-78535-582-0

Neglected or Misunderstood
The Radical Feminism of Shulamith Firestone
Victoria Margree
An interrogation of issues surrounding gender, biology, sexuality, work and technology, and the ways in which our imaginations continue to be in thrall to ideologies of maternity and the nuclear family.
Paperback: 978-1-78535-539-4 ebook: 978-1-78535-540-0

How to Dismantle the NHS in 10 Easy Steps (Second Edition)
Youssef El-Gingihy
The story of how your NHS was sold off and why you will have to buy private health insurance soon. A new expanded second edition with chapters on junior doctors' strikes and government blueprints for US-style healthcare.
Paperback: 978-1-78904-178-1 ebook: 978-1-78904-179-8

Digesting Recipes
The Art of Culinary Notation
Susannah Worth
A recipe is an instruction, the imperative tone of the expert, but this constraint can offer its own kind of potential. A recipe need not be a domestic trap but might instead offer escape — something to fantasise about or aspire to.
Paperback: 978-1-78279-860-6 ebook: 978-1-78279-859-0

Most titles are published in paperback and as an ebook. Paperbacks are available in traditional bookshops. Both print and ebook formats are available online.
Follow us at:
https://www.facebook.com/ZeroBooks
https://twitter.com/Zer0Books
https://www.instagram.com/zero.books